T0334410

BACKSEAT QUARTERBACK

BACKSEAT QUARTERBACK

by Perian Conerly

University Press of Mississippi / *Jackson*

First published in 1963 by Doubleday & Company, Inc. www.
upress.state.ms.us

The University Press of Mississippi is a member of the
Association of American University Presses.

Library of Congress Cataloging-in-Publication Data
Conerly, Perian.
Backseat quarterback/ by Perian Conerly.
p. cm
Originally published: Garden City, N.Y. : Doubleday, 1963.
ISBN 978-1-4968-4952-6 (trade paperback)
1. Football-United States-Miscellanea. I. Title.

GV959.C6 2003
796.332'02-dc21   2003043275

British Library Cataloging-in-Publication Data available

To Benjamin Taylor Collier (1891–1957)

Who would have thought this the wittiest, cleverest, most informative piece of writing he had ever read—with the austere impartiality that only the father of a girl-child can muster.

And to Mother, Gladys Whiting Collier (1895–1997)

Who in her 102nd year was still the prettiest (really!), brightest, sweetest lady I have ever known.

And of course to Charles (1921–1996)

Simply the best.

CONTENTS

FOREWORD

When Perian Conerly came up with the idea, back in the early '60s, of writing a book many friends of her husband Charlie Conerly quite frankly wondered what she was going to write about. The way we saw it, Peri was one of the guys and over the years she had been present and often actively part of some real "serious fun." Obviously, we should never have worried. Peri not only didn't "out" us with any tabloidish revelations of some of our late night travels, she truly captured what it was like being the wife of one of the NFL's greatest players in the greatest city in the world at a time when the game itself was just sprouting wings.

Charlie and Peri had been on the scene some five years before I came to the Giants in 1952. They had been tough years in the sense that Charlie, as the Giants quarterback, had struggled to make a mediocre team look as though it belonged on the field. Charlie suffered both physically and very quietly emotionally. Without the support of Perian, I'm sure he would have packed it in and moved back home to his beloved Clarksdale, Mississippi, and become a gentleman farmer. After all, this was a guy who had fought his way as a combat marine across the South Pacific, watching buddies die and never knowing when the "next one" would be his. He frankly didn't need the abuse he took in his first few years both from an unknowing press and two-bit hecklers in the bleachers of the old Polo Grounds. Thankfully for Perian, the Giants, yours truly, and millions of football fans, Charlie toughed it out and became the key man for the Giants as they climbed the ladder to a NFL Championship.

Charlie and I were roommates on the Giants for nine years. We had some good times and bad times on the field, but we had mostly great times off the field. New York City during our "run" with the Giants was the greatest city in which a professional athlete could hope to play. Unlike today, most of our players lived in the City and loved the proximity to all the Big Apple had to offer.

Perian, in *Backseat Quarterback*, captures the true essence of what it was like to be a Giant in NYC during the relatively innocent time of the late '40s, '50s, and early '60s. She mixed together a great reading blend of football; what it was like to be the wife of a football legend; and a close-up view of New York City's glittery night life, including Toots Shor's, P. J. Clarke's, Eddie Condon's, Mike Manuche's, and many other wonderful places that have come and gone.

For me, it brings back fabulous memories of great times with both Peri and my best friend, Charlie Conerly, as well as a very special time in all our lives. Enjoy!!

Frank Gifford
February 2003

PROLOGUE
On Naming a Book

Though a novice in the field of letters, I have long been aware that the title of a book has a great deal to do with its ultimate success. Had Gibbon given *The Decline and Fall of the Roman Empire* a more imaginative title like *Shame of a City* or *The Sex Kittens Visit Rome*, I'm convinced that the work would have become a classic. Admittedly, there might not have been an appreciable increase in the number of people who actually *read* the book. But the number of people who *bought* it would no doubt have been infinitely greater—until the word got around, anyway.

With this precept in mind, I gave considerable attention to the selection of a title for *my* book. After some thought, I came up with the possibility which might appeal to that segment of readers with a fondness for gore: *Massacre on Sunday: A Searing Indictment of Pro Football*. But I reluctantly dismissed the idea, fearing it might arouse the ire of my ilk. And my ilk runs to large people, awesome when angry.

I next dwelt on two others: *Please Don't Eat the Quarterback* and *The Quarterback and I*. Friends convinced me that both had a too-familiar ring.

A predilection for puns led to *The Passing Years*. I scratched that one when a neighbor suggested that it sounded like the title of a treatise on senility. (I had no wish to give Conerly detractors the opportunity of hinting that such an implication might be entirely appropriate.)

The best suggestion came from a friend who has a flair for salesmanship. The cover would be emblazoned with a four-color picture of me in a filmy negligee. The title: *My Thirteen Years as a Pro*. We agreed, however, that the idea was best suited for the paperback edition. This approach alone would sell a million copies to men in a hurry to catch trains, planes, or whatever. But I couldn't figure out a way to keep my mother from seeing it.

The next idea came to me one night in a dream. (We had had venison hassenpfeffer for supper.) What it was, was *What It Is, Is Football*. I thought it had a certain homespun touch. My advisors agreed that the title had distinct possibilities, but one (a local lawyer) pointed out that there might be difficulty in coming to terms with Andy Griffith.

After discarding a host of similarly impractical notions, I reconsidered the title of my newspaper column. Kyle Rote's wife, Betty, had been partly responsible for its origin several years ago. I was getting close to it anyhow, with *Rumble Seat Quarterback*. But Betty pointed out that the word "rumble" has a connotation for today's teenagers that is somewhat different than the one it has for us, and sloppy readers might assume somehow that sports figures condone juvenile delinquency. She then suggested *Backseat Quarterback*.

I think that I should elaborate on the meaning of the title. Though a vague takeoff on "backseat driver," it is not intended to imply that I have any major part in planning the field strategy of the New York Football Giants. Like any fan, I have definite opinions on how things should be handled, but my constructive abetments are confined principally to dispassionate postgame comments. ("The next time that big linebacker tackles you after the ball is thrown, I wish you'd ask Rosie Brown to straighten *him* out!")

Instead, the title is designed to suggest that I take a backseat where my husband's business is concerned, but am ever lurking in the background, eager to compensate for his unfortunate character traits. Like modesty. I always try to be on hand when Charlie is being interviewed, for instance. You see, I know that when the reporter asks: "Have you ever played any sport besides football?" Charlie will say, "No."

This flagrant disregard of fact is based principally on inherent modesty, but I have a feeling that a desire for brevity—and silence—also enters the picture. The sooner the reporter leaves, the sooner Charles can get back to

To Kill a Mockingbird. (Now *there's* a title!) Since reticence has never been one of my strong points, I quickly inject a patronizing "Oh, *come* now . . ." and bombard the writer with a documentation of Charlie's prowess. I confide brightly that he, like many athletes, excelled in several sports. For instance, Charlie hit .467 as an outfielder his senior year at Ole Miss and consequently received several attractive offers to enter professional baseball. He played basketball and tennis in high school, broke 80 three months after he took up golf, bowled over two hundred the fourth time he tried the game; and despite almost total lack of practice these last fifteen years, still hasn't lost his eye with a pool cue.

Ignoring my spouse's embarrassed and dark displeasure (now being dramatized by a faint chorus of knuckle-popping), I recall aloud that an informal baseball team which once barn-stormed the hometown area still bore his childhood nick-name (The Roaches)—some twenty years after he and a group of friends organized the we'll-play-anybody team. Then, to return to the subject at hand, I throw in for good measure that Charlie still holds or shares every single passing record in the archives of both the Ole Miss Rebels and the New York Giants.

Strange—but the Frontseat Quarterback seems to make every effort to see that I am off the premises whenever an inquiring reporter comes to call.

Therefore, in retaliation for all those surreptitious interviews and all the times I was glared into silence when I fain would speak, behold! *Backseat Quarterback:* An *on*-the-premises account of the delights and disappointments that have occurred in an eighth of a century with my favorite sport. (I also plan to mention *his* favorite sport: football.)

BACKSEAT
QUARTERBACK

{1}

THE ROAD TO NEW YORK

By nature I am extremely optimistic. The kind, for instance, who assumes the laundry is saving all those socks they fail to return and, the first time I call in person, will present me with a boxful of mates to the boxful of mismates I have at home.

Now you must admit it. *That* is optimism.

I am also something of an extrovert. I talk to people. Frequently I talk to people who are not talking to me, a habit which makes my rather reticent husband (not to mention the people) terribly nervous. For instance, if a stranger standing within earshot asks his companion what time it is and the friend is not wearing a watch, I simply cannot restrain myself from imparting helpfully, "It's nine thirty-five." And if my spouse is not close enough to give me that copyrighted withering look of his, I explain that I know it is *exactly* nine thirty-five because I set my watch just as "Maverick" was going off the air a short time before, but that I really don't care much for the show since Jim Garner quit, and . . .

It is therefore somewhat startling that as the train approached New York's Pennsylvania Station that night back in 1949, I underwent a most disconcerting metamorphosis. Optimism and extroversion vanished. I began to regard the seatmates with whom I had been chatting in a new and suspicious light. I was suddenly assailed with doubt: The gray-haired man across from me was not an insurance salesman, as he had said. More likely he was the mastermind of a white slave ring. Just the type. So innocent-looking. I avoided his gaze.

I had *heard things* about the City.

And the well-dressed lady to my left who had admired my new purse earlier. Very probably she intended to snatch it and run as soon as the train stopped. I tightened my grasp.

In a surge of uncertainty, I began to experience that gloomy, empty feeling of the traveler who is expecting to be met on arrival—but isn't. I'm sure I told him Thursday on the phone. Yes, I'm positive I said Thursday . . . I think. I was pretty excited at the time. Suppose there is another train station in New York besides Penn Station, and he goes to the wrong one! I immediately dismissed this possibility as too ridiculous for serious consideration. Why would *one* town bother to build *two* railway stations? I chuckled audibly at my foolish misgivings. Suddenly an inner voice from the distant past intoned: *Grand Cen—tral Sta—shun!* Of course! There was once a whole radio show about it—on Saturday mornings right after "Let's Pretend." I consoled myself with the thought that I still had a 50–50 chance he would choose the right station. Pretty good odds. (Except in those movies when the doctor closes the door quietly, shakes his head and says, "She has a 50–50 chance." They always die.)

Suppose he doesn't meet me. What in the world would I do? I reflected solemnly for a moment. Of course! First, I'll have him paged at Grand Cen—tral Sta—shun. If they can't locate him, I'll call the Giant office. *They'll* know what to do. Plan B evaporated as I looked at my watch. Small chance that the office of the New York Football Giants would be open at eight o'clock at night! "How did I ever get into this?" I wailed half-aloud. The white slaver and the purse-snatcher looked up wonderingly. I lowered my eyes and sank into reverie. Here I am. Twelve hundred miles from home. All alone. Surrounded by questionable characters. "How did I ever get into this?" I repeated. And answered by remembering.

It all started in August of 1947. I had just returned from attending summer school at the University of Wyoming, where my eldest sister was a member of the faculty. The joys of supplementing my schooling had, I'm afraid, been incidental to the obvious advantages of attending a co-educational institution where the "co-s" were outnumbered by the "eds" approximately ten to one during the summer session. I was loath to leave this westerly Utopia, it is true, but coming home is invariably the best part of any trip.

Eager to catch up with the rush of events in Clarksdale, Mississippi (population about 15,000 at that time) during my absence, I proceeded to the municipal swimming pool, which was customarily the gathering place for the college set in the summertime. There, I sat on the edge of the pool chatting with one of the life guards—a boy who had been in my high school class. Since he had a heavy date that night and since I had worked as a life guard for the three previous summers, he had almost convinced me to take over his duties at the pool so that he could pick up his girl at six o'clock instead of waiting until the pool closed at nine. His pleas were taking effect when Farley Salmon, another contemporary of mine, ambled up, accompanied by a man he introduced as Charles Albert Conerly, Jr. Farley, Charlie, and I strolled over to the Coke stand, leaving the lovelorn life guard with his problem unresolved.

Now, of course I knew who Charlie was. Anyone in town able to read a newspaper could hardly escape knowing. He had been Clarksdale's star halfback in his high school days and was currently the bright hope of the 1947 Ole Miss (University of Mississippi) football team. Of course I knew *him*. However, when he was graduated from high school, I was in the eighth grade. So it is understandable that our paths had not crossed socially.

I was immediately taken with his dark good looks and engaging shyness. And he had lean, low-slung lines peculiar to athletes and Cadillacs. I have always been partial to both.

In the South nearly all boys play football. "Going out for the team" (whether making it or not) is a sort of prestige symbol. Football players, therefore, were no novelty to me.

But one five years older than I? Now that was something else again . . .

The attraction was evidently reciprocal, for Charlie asked me to double-date with mutual friends that evening, and we continued to see each other almost every night until the pre-season practice sessions called him to Ole Miss several weeks later. I tied up a few loose ends by fulfilling obligations accepted prior to our meeting, then confined my attentions exclusively to Him.

I was a junior at Mississippi State College for Women that fall; he was a senior at the University in Oxford, some ninety miles distant. Charlie's college career had been interrupted by a three-year stint in the Marine Corps, a fact that explains why I was now only one year behind him in school. Since neither the temptation nor the opportunity to spend money had presented itself on Guam and Iwo Jima during the war, he saved most of his corporal's salary and bought a brand-new car as soon as postwar models were available. My All-American and his baby blue Buick were a familiar sight on the MSCW campus that fall.

Until Charlie and I began "keeping company," I was a fan of the Mississippi State Bulldogs, traditional rivals of the Ole Miss Rebels. This allegiance had been inspired principally by proximity. (State is located only twenty-eight miles from MSCW—exactly sixty-two dating miles closer than Ole Miss.) Nevertheless, I had little trouble in shifting my loyalty and managed to see "Chunkin' Charlie" play in three games that fall. Incidentally, in the South the colloquialism for "throw" is "chunk"—not "chuck." Therefore he is "Chunkin' Charlie" in Southern newspapers; "Chuckin' Charlie" or, heaven forefend, "Chuckin' Chuck" in Northern publications.

In pre-season predictions, few experts had picked Mississippi to finish higher than tenth in the field of twelve Southeastern Conference teams. Several optimists went out on a limb and ranked the Rebels ninth. The prognosticators had not reckoned with a phrase that was to haunt the dreams of Ole Miss's opponents in 1947: "Conerly to Poole—complete!" With Charlie chunking the ball and Barney catching it, Ole Miss won its very first conference championship!

Charlie also won the collegiate passing title in 1947. In fact, he set a new national record by completing 133 of 232 passes that season. It is likely that he could have put the mark out of reach, perhaps forever, were it not for the fact that he saw little action in the second half of the last three games. Mississippi piled up substantial leads early in those contests, and Coach John Vaught wisely gave next year's corps of hopefuls the benefit of combat experience. When Ole Miss met Chattanooga (the only so-called breather on the Ole Miss schedule), Charlie donned "civilian" clothes and watched the second half of the game from the bench.

Charlie's outstanding success as a passer tended to overshadow his talent for various other phases of the game. But things being the way they were, I could rattle off his 1947 statistics as fast as a blasé fifth-grader can say the pledge of allegiance to the flag. He passed for 18 touchdowns and scored 9 more afoot. He gained 1366 yards through the air, and 417 on the ground in 104 attempts. He punted 58 times for a 40.2 average, and as one writer put it, "defended with consummate skill on every occasion."

December 3, 1947, was proclaimed "Charlie Conerly Day" in Clarksdale. Fans from all over the state gathered to bestow plaudits on Charles and a new Chevrolet on his mother. (He could not accept so valuable a gift himself with baseball eligibility remaining.) I was unable to attend the celebration because it took place on a Wednesday. (MSCW girls were allowed to make out-of-town trips only on weekends, except in extraordinary circumstances.) Dean Keirn had the reputation of being "a sucker for a love story," and I was hopeful of convincing her that mine was a special case. However, she said she couldn't let me go unless Charlie and I were actually engaged. As badly as I wanted to go, I couldn't bring myself to stretch the truth quite that far. Besides, I was afraid the next time she saw him on campus, she would rush up and congratulate him, thereby exposing my presumptuous deception to both and causing my untimely demise by mortification.

On Christmas night he asked me to marry him. I said yes—with a reservation. I would have to finish college. I could not disappoint my parents by quitting with only a year and a half to go, I explained, neglecting to mention a not-so-altruistic reason for wishing to graduate. I liked school. The next year I would be a senior. The thought of passing up the delectation (commonly enjoyed by fourth-year students) of being held in awe by adoring freshmen was out of the question. Besides, I had been elected editor-in-chief of the MSCW *Spectator*. "Never know when newspaper experience will come in handy," I rationalized.

Charles grudgingly agreed to wait.

Doubtlessly influenced by the pessimistic pre-season predictions, University officials accepted a bowl bid before the season even started. They agreed to meet an opponent to be selected later in the first "annual" Delta Bowl to be played in Memphis on January 1. (The last was played a year later.) Winning the Southeastern Conference championship subsequently brought offers to appear in more venerable post-season games—the Sugar Bowl, among others—but Ole Miss honored the prior commitment.

The first day of 1948 was cold, with the temperature at twenty-five degrees, and a bone-chilling thirty-five-mile-per-hour wind raking those hardy, half-frozen spectators who stayed to see Ole Miss defeat Texas Christian University, 13–9. Even a flu-inspired fever of 103 degrees failed to keep me warm. (I had surreptitiously shaken the thermometer down to normal that morning so Mother wouldn't make me stay home.) I managed to paste a smile on my face during the victory banquet that night, then took to my sickbed for a week.

In June of 1948 Charlie signed a five-year contract with the Giants in preference to accepting Branch Rickey's much-publicized offer of $100,000 to join the Brooklyn Dodgers of the upstart All-America Football Conference.

Mr. Rickey howled in print that free enterprise was being imperiled when a boy could be persuaded to accept one offer so vastly "inferior" to another. Charlie replied via the *New York Times:* "The Brooklyn offer came only after the Dodgers were sure I had decided to play with the Giants. I never seriously considered playing with the Dodgers and told scout Wid Matthews so when he approached me. I guess they announced that offer to make themselves look good and make me feel sorry for myself. I don't."

As a matter of fact, Charlie's mother recalls that his decision to play with the Giants was made long before they ever heard of him. One day when he was about eight years old Charles burst into the kitchen. "Mother! Guess what I am going to be when I grow up."

Mrs. Conerly remembers that she was a little startled by this because Charles was never a particularly fanciful child.

"Guess!" Charles repeated.

"A policeman? A fireman?"

"No, ma'am. A professional football player with the New York Giants."

"You mean a *baseball* player," she corrected. Charles seemed to spend every waking moment either playing baseball or throwing a ball against the house and catching it. (And it is probable she had never heard of *professional* football, since the NFL was only about as old as Charlie at that time.)

"No ma'am," he insisted. "Football . . . but I might play baseball too."

"He never would tell me where he got the idea," Mrs. Conerly said, "but from then on the Giants were 'his' team."

In discussing the decision with me, Charlie reasoned that the Giants were an established team, members of a league that had been on the sports scene a long time. "They'll probably be around a while longer, and who knows what will happen to the new league . . ." (Author's note: The Brooklyn club was disbanded when the All-America Conference folded after the 1949 season.)

We were sitting on my front porch that day swinging in the glider. Since we had become officially engaged a few weeks earlier, our conversation turned to the future. Charlie beamed enthusiastically as he outlined his plans for us: "With the bonus the Giants gave me, I made a down payment on 225 acres south of town. I think it will be a good investment. Dad has always wanted to raise cotton, and will manage it for me. And with the first year's salary, we can buy a home."

I just smiled foolishly and stole an admiring glance at my engagement ring.

Charlie left for All-Star training camp the first of August 1948. I drove to Chicago with his parents for the game on August 20. He left the next day to join the Giants, and I did not see him again until the middle of December. The separation was dreadful, but despite it, Charles managed to be voted NFL Rookie of the Year and I managed to get the *Spectator* out on time.

We were married on the hottest day in June 1949, three weeks after my graduation.

In recalling that event, I murmured a fervent prayer that the mishaps which occurred prior to and during the wedding did not portend similar confusion for the years of marriage to follow. The ceremony took place in the First Methodist Church in Clarksdale. Six of the nine groomsmen had been Charlie's teammates at Ole Miss. My five attendants included high school and college friends summoned from around the nation and one of my sisters (the other was eight months pregnant).

The night before the wedding, one of the bridesmaids discovered that she had left the sash to her gown at home—in Evansville, Indiana. After a vain attempt to match the pale yellow taffeta in the local department stores early next morning, she made a frantic call to her father, who arrived by train with the sash thirty minutes before the kick-off.

The morning of the wedding, the elder of Charlie's two sisters slipped over to a neighbor's house and telephoned me to report that I had forgotten to invite the Conerly family to the wedding reception! Immediately I leaped into the car and sped out to the farm to rectify this monumental *faux pas*, shuddering all the way in the thought that I had blown the whole in-law bit before I even got into the family. Fortunately Mrs. Conerly, senior, possesses a forgiving nature.

As my father was dressing for the wedding that evening, he discovered there was no tie among his borrowed finery. We were about to tie a black sock around his neck when someone suggested that the two young bachelor brothers who lived around the corner surely would have one. They did.

Then as we were walking out the door, church-bound, the buckle on Mother's slipper came off. Another short delay ensued while she dashed back to sew it on.

The assortment of inquisitive strangers who popped in and out of the house at the height of the confusion were reporters, I learned later. I also seem to remember that Mother exhibited slight annoyance over the fact that in several papers the wedding notice appeared not in the society section, but on the sports page.

At the church, Daddy and I waited in an anteroom with my nephew and niece (ages four and two) who were also scheduled to participate. "You go ahead and sit out front," I had told their mother optimistically, "I can make them behave." The youngsters were quiet for awhile, but soon became bored by the prolonged delay. Rod began turning somersaults on the floor. As Daddy jerked him upright, Rebecca began to turn somersaults. As Daddy pursued her, Rod began to throw straight pins into the fan, which was aimed at the perspiring bride. In order to put a stop to this little game, Daddy had to release Rebecca, who immediately resumed her acrobatics. And so on. Since I was immobilized (my train was draped over three chairs to keep it from getting soiled) I could render only vocal assistance.

Daddy finally gritted his teeth. "We'll just lock the door and leave them in here. I'll not have them ruining your wedding!" He relented at the last minute after I pleaded tearily that "Teeny" (the pregnant sister) had spent *so* much time making Rod's little white suit and Rebecca's dress (a miniature copy of the bridesmaids' dresses) . . .

The last bridesmaid and groomsman disappeared down the aisle, followed by Daddy's now-angelic grandchildren. As the organ began the wedding march, Daddy and I waited nervously in the vestibule for the "ready signal." The Chief of Operations (a friend of Mother's) dashed up, and we took a step forward. "No, not yet!" she whispered hoarsely, "The groomsmen forgot to unroll the white carpet, and it's still piled up at the altar! Ben, you're the only one left . . ."

The organ boomed "Here Comes the Bride" a little more insistently, it seemed. As Daddy marched down the aisle *alone,* a buzz ran through the crowd: *She's fainted! . . . She's changed her mind! . . .* Anxious eyes darted from the bride's father, apparently bent on his grim mission, to the soon-to-be-disappointed bridegroom. Meanwhile, back at the altar . . . despite a deep golfer's tan, Charlie paled noticeably (so friends told me later).

His chore completed, Daddy returned to try once more to give me away. Just as we turned the corner and started down the main aisle, a woman photographer in the balcony fell off a ladder. She didn't quite make it over the railing, but the commotion was sufficient to draw all eyes away from the radiant, semiconscious bride.

When it was all over, Mother, who can always manage to find a bright spot in any cloudy situation, said, "Didn't the church look lovely! And so many people were there."

"I'm sorry, Mother," I had to admit, "but I didn't *see* the church, and the only two people I remember were Charles and Lillie." Lillie was my old colored nurse. She carried me home from the hospital in her arms when I was eight days old and remained my confidante until she retired many years later. Lillie had admonished me the day before the wedding: "I'm getting dressed up fit to kill to see My Gold Baby get married [I had long blond curls as a child]. Now you look up in the balcony and wave at your old Lillie." I did.

The honeymoon ended abruptly with Charles's departure for the Giant training camp, located that year in Saranac Lake, New York. A bride of six weeks, I took a rather dim view of the accepted procedure whereby players' wives remain at home until the start of the regular season. But I decided to wait at least one year before overthrowing the heartless Giant regime, and grudgingly fidgeted away my nine-week widowhood in Clarksdale, writing pitiful "I miss you" letters to my personal quarterback so far away. At long, long last, departure day grew near.

I recalled Mother's apprehension at the thought of her youngest daughter blithely setting out to begin a life so foreign to anything either of us had ever known. "Your daddy and I spent a wonderful vacation there once, but I'm told that New York can be a cold and lonesome place in which to live," she worried aloud, then added hastily, "But I'm sure it won't be that way for you."

"Well, if there's nothing else to do, I'll just sleep," I had replied. That pronouncement seemed to assuage her fears. (Having been acquainted with me for twenty-two years at that time, she was well aware of my stunning aptitude in that field.)

And so—on to the city. I wondered what living in New York *would* be like. "I hope the other wives like me. Wonder if I'll get to see any celebrities . . ."

"Penn Station!" the conductor sang out. I counted my belongings. Purse, coat, train case, two suitcases. Five. I beamed a weak farewell smile at my traveling companions—on the off chance they were legitimate—and bolted for the door. Making arrangements with the redcap to meet me in the station with the luggage, I shouldered my way through the crowd, looking neither to the right nor to the left.

A man spoke to me and I started noticeably. "I believe you dropped this scarf," he repeated.

"Oh, yes, yes, thank you." My voice was curiously high-pitched. Just then I saw Charlie striding toward me, a broad, crooked grin on his face. And suddenly the big town wasn't such a bad place after all. (I later discovered the crookedness was designed to conceal a gap. He had been relieved of a tooth in the previous week's exhibition game.)

As we were claiming my baggage a man passing by smiled and tipped his hat.

"Good-by, Mr. McCormick, and good luck!" I called merrily.

"Who was that?" Charles wanted to know.

"Oh, just a nice old man I sat with on the train."

{2}

THE PROS

Perhaps it is totally insignificant that what is generally considered the beginning of the modern era of professional football coincides with the arrival of Charles Conerly on the scene. Nonetheless, during the years 1948–62 we have seen the game grow from a stuttering stepchild into the darling of the sports world. Extensive television coverage no doubt greatly hastened its acceptance as a major sport, and today's children grow up with the game. Any sports-minded fourth-grader can quote the vital statistics of every prominent player in the league. By contrast, Charlie played in the first professional game he ever saw.

The increasing popularity of the sport is evidenced by the fact that each succeeding year attendance records are shattered throughout the league. As a result, owners are happy and players' salaries are larger.

An excellent barometer of the warming romance between the public and pro football is the amount each player receives for participation in the championship game (based on the paid attendance plus sale of radio and television rights). In 1951, Detroit and Cleveland set a high with $2274 going to each member of the winning team (Detroit) and $1712 to the loser. Compare these figures with the cut of the 1961 participants. Each Green Bay Packer took home $5195 and each Giant $3340—a record despite the fact that the number of shares voted by each club was unusually large. While cheering for the home team in the good old college fashion at these post-season affairs, we wives cannot dispel the materialistic thought: A one-point difference on the scoreboard at the end of the game can make a $1855 difference in the size of Papa's paycheck.

All phases of the game have been affected by change during our tenure. Women are notorious for radical innovations in styles of dress, but a snapshot of rookie Conerly sporting the close-fitting leather helmet universally worn in 1948 would evoke as hearty a chuckle as a picture of me wearing the ankle-trailing skirt of that year's "new look." Today's plastic helmets, lined with sponge rubber and fitted with webbing which acts as a shock absorber, afford far superior protection.

Sponge rubber has also replaced the bulkier stuffing formerly used in various body pads, thus lightening the player's load and allowing him increased speed and maneuverability. The use of lightweight miracle fabrics in jerseys and pants adds greatly to his comfort.

Ever since the inception of protective equipment, "bird-cage" face masks have been the trademark of the interior linemen. The crisscross of leather-covered wire tends to inhibit the wearer's lateral vision, a nuisance which seldom impairs the efficiency of a guard or tackle charging straight ahead. However, such a device was unfeasible for use by the passer, his receivers, and by pass defenders—who have the common need of seeing in all directions at once.

The recent advent of practical face masks which provide the wearer protection without restricting his vision has been a boon in curtailing face injuries, once common. Charlie points wistfully to the happy fact that the younger players in the league generally possess the facial contours with which Nature—not an errant elbow—endowed them. This observation is substantiated by Dr. Francis J. Sweeny, Giant team physician for thirty years, who estimates that injuries to nose, mouth, face, jaw, and eye have decreased by 50 percent since 1955, the year the face bar was adopted. He recalls that in the maskless days nose fractures were accepted philosophically as an occupational hazard and occurred at the rate of about one a game or ten a year. In a pre-season exhibition game last season Charlie suffered what a wire-service release described (rather loosely, I thought) as "a comfortable nose fracture." Dr. Sweeny stated that the freakish accident (a karate-like blow which slammed between the double bar of his mask) was the first broken nose sustained by a Giant player in over four years!

It is also significant that most of the younger men on the squad are not even acquainted with Dr. Croker, Giant team dentist, who once barely found time during the football season for ministering to his regular patients.

"I guess I'm the only one in the organization who is not in favor of the face guard," Dr. Croker says with a twinkle. "Before it came into use, I ordinarily had several nice visits each season with nearly every player on the team. Nowadays only a few of the older boys even know who I am. I miss being in the middle of things."

Considering that the marked decrease in the incidence of facial disfiguration is attributable to the face guards, it is not surprising that every Giant player on the 1961 squad expressed reluctance to play without one. In fact, only two players of the more than five hundred in the NFL eschew this protection—Bobby Layne (Steelers) and Jess Richardson (Eagles). A foolhardy idiosyncrasy, their Giant colleagues agree.

It may be interesting to note that the face of the pro football scene itself was altered to some degree by the players' fondness for the face guard. A player-owner controversy over abandoning the device after one year's trial provided the impetus for the formation of the Players' Association—the NFL version of the workingman's union. On discovering that the forerunner of the present face bar (a lucite band) was not shatterproof, the owners forbade its use. Loosely organized player agitation protesting the face guard ban resulted in the adoption of a substitute, the unbreakable bar used currently.

United by the dispute and awakened to the potential value of an organization committed to protecting the rights of the players, a vanguard of veteran NFL performers set about to establish a players' association. The founders agreed that, though most owners treat players fairly, this relationship should assume consistent and legally binding proportions. Charlie and I personally had no complaints regarding our employers. We endorsed the idea as beneficial to the whole, but were mere followers in the movement—typical let-*them*-do-it participants. However, successful projects generally inspire a good bit of "we-ing" in retrospect. Therefore, we of the Players' Association point with pride to the principal accomplishments of the association since 1956: Inclusion of an injury clause in the player contracts. Adoption of a hospitalization and life insurance program for all players. A minimum salary. Establishment of a pension fund.

Rule changes in the National Football League during and since 1948 have not wielded a drastic effect on the game, but a few are notable. The league limit on the number of players each team may carry has vacillated between thirty-two and thirty-six in the past fourteen years. During the 1960 season the roster limit was raised temporarily to thirty-eight, presumably in order to soften the hardship of permitting the new Minnesota Vikings to form a team by selecting three players from a list of twelve "expendables" submitted by each established NFL squad. The number was set officially at thirty-six for the 1961 season.

The use of an artificial tee for kick-offs was initiated in 1948. The old rule required that the ball be held in place for the kicker by another player, as is still the case in point after touchdown and field goal attempts. However, if he desires, the kicker still may request the services of a "live" holder in kicking off.

Incidentally, the NFL rule book continues to be cluttered with notations to the effect that the drop-kick method may be employed in any kicking situation (in lieu of punts, kick-offs, and field goal and extra point attempts). In thirteen years on the pro scene I have never seen a drop kick executed. The official definition (quoted here for the benefit of the younger generation) is "a kick by a kicker who drops the ball and kicks it as or immediately after the ball touches the ground."

In days gone by, the repertoire of every accomplished kicker contained a respectable drop kick. However, when the shape of the ball was changed years ago (it was elongated to facilitate forward passing) kickers abandoned the method because they could no longer count on a true rebound. Perhaps it was they who originated that philosophical phrase, "Oh, well, that's the way the ball bounces!"

Prior to the snap of the ball, movement by an interior lineman after taking a three-point stance was ruled as illegal motion in 1956. This stipulation speeded up the game by reducing the number of offside penalties which formerly halted the action with aggravating regularity. Previously, opposing linemen would endeavor to draw each other offside by feinting movement in advance of the snap from center. Now they must remain immobile after getting set on the line.

In the early 1950s, the general practice of designating specific numerals to certain positions was made compulsory—presumably to make player identification simpler for the spectator. Quarterbacks were thenceforth required to wear a number from 1 to 19; halfbacks, a number in the 20s or 40s; fullbacks in the 30s; centers in the 50s; guards in the 60s; tackles in the 70s; and ends in the 80s. Players already wearing numerals contrary to the system when the ruling went into effect were allowed to retain their old numbers. For this reason, Charlie's uniform bears No. 42 instead of the low numbers assigned to present-day quarterbacks. (He brought number 42 from Ole Miss, where he was a passing halfback.)

The most widely known difference between college and pro football was eliminated, or rather mitigated, in 1956. Previously a pro runner downed by an opponent, if able to break loose before the whistle sounded, was permitted to run or crawl for additional yardage. Injuries caused by defenders piling on the inert ball carrier to make certain he did not get up and run reached such alarming proportions that the rules committee amended the regulation to allow only a player who had slipped and fallen inadvertently, and had not been touched by an opponent, to continue his forward progress.

During the first few years after the rule went into effect the rate of "unnecessary roughness" penalties soared above the norm. In the heat of battle, tacklers unconsciously reverted to the hold-'em-down tactics so long a part of the defensive repertoire. In recent seasons the pendulum has swung the other way. I have noticed numerous instances wherein ball carriers new to the professional ranks failed to make extra yardage because they were accustomed to college rules. Having fallen (usually because of poor footing) in the open field, they just lie there waiting for the whistle to blow—forgetting they could rise and continue running.

Though the general switch to the T-formation occurred prior to our modern era, two NFL teams still clung to the outmoded single wing (or to its first cousin, the A-formation) when Charlie joined the pros. The Giants under Steve Owen did not make the changeover until 1949, Charlie's sophomore year. (The last team to junk the single wing, the Steelers, did so in 1952.) Al Sherman, a dedicated student of the science of football who had seen limited service as a left-handed passer with the Philadelphia Eagles, was tapped to install the system. (Al was destined to become head coach of the Giants in 1961.)

Charlie passed from the tailback (left halfback) spot in college and therefore had never played the T-quarterback position. Despite the long hours of practice required to learn the mechanics of the formation (such things as backpedaling in order to reach the passing pocket; the delicate foot and hand movements required in spinning to hand off and in faking; the quickness and the consistency of timing necessary to place the ball in the carrier's hands or stomach in exactly the same manner each time), Charlie was happy with the change. He felt the system itself was superior because of the direct snap from center—a maneuver which affords more deception, more variety of attack, and quicker-hitting plays. He also realized that his own career would undoubtedly be lengthened because the T-quarterback is rarely called on to run with the ball or to block.

Innovations in T-formation strategy during the past decade principally concern alignment. Increased use of flankers and of the spread formation typify today's pro offense. The 4–3–2–2 defense has become the standard for the pros, replacing the 5–3–3, 7–4, etc.

The traditional twelve-game schedule was increased to fourteen beginning with the 1961 season, a change occasioned by the addition of two new teams to the NFL—the Dallas Cowboys in 1960 and the Minnesota Vikings in 1961. The league is divided into eastern and western conferences of seven teams each. Each club continues to play twice against the other (six) members of its conference and two games against teams belonging to the other conference.

The inter-conference pairings are set up on what might be described as a lenient rotation basis, for the league commissioner may use his discretion in making the schedule as interesting as possible. For example, he will give particular attention to what he considers are natural rivalries. Though the Giants played a division-spanning game against the Green Bay Packers as recently as 1959, the teams were scheduled for a rematch in 1961. It is probable that both pairings were designed to capitalize on the interest occasioned by the fact that Packer head coach Vinnie Lombardi labored for five years as Giant offensive coach.

To me the most heart-warming trend in the years 1948–62 concerns the enlightened attitude of the general public toward the game of pro football, and more especially toward the men who play it. The professional football player today is far from being the brawny, brainless specimen popularly associated with the early game. He is almost always college-educated, and the additional polish acquired by extensive travel and public appearances (including those on radio and television) endow him with poise equal to that of an above-average businessman. The mental gymnastics required of him would make many a C.P.A. shake his head in dismay. For example, considering all the variations of the basic formations, the quarterback has in his repertoire about a thousand different plays. And Charlie says the defensive maneuvers are even more complicated. The slow-witted brute has disappeared from the scene.

The man on the street is now aware that the game requires a mind as well as a body. Consequently, business firms in increasing numbers are recognizing the wisdom of adding to their public relations staffs these personable, educated, poised young men who possess, in addition, a built-in foot-in-the-door.

Lucrative endorsements have become more frequent. Manufacturers have come to realize that the sporting public not only knows, for example, who Sam Huff is—but seems to care what brand of gasoline he puts in his car. It is significant that linemen, once considered a necessary but not a particularly colorful part of football, are coming into their rightful share of the sideline gravy. This fact surely indicates that Mr. John Q. has developed a keener understanding of the game as a whole.

Such understanding, coupled with a growing interest in the players and their wives as people, has almost eliminated a discomfort we once considered an occupational hazard: the embarrassing situation born of misinformation. Well-meaning citizens of Greenville, Mississippi, no longer ask All-Pro safety Jimmy Patton: "Where are you stationed now, Jim Boy?"—assuming that his periodic absences from the home town could mean only that he was in the army. What else? Today the local barber or the milkman or the preacher is more likely to ask: "Say, Jim, is Big Daddy Lipscomb really as big as he looks on television?"

Then there was the annual report of a friend of ours: "The rumors are flying again," she would announce. "Just thought you ought to know. I overheard Mrs. So-and-So in the beauty parlor yesterday telling her hairdresser, 'Well, he's left her again. This time for good. I have it on very good authority that she has instituted divorce proceedings. Can't much blame Perian—the way Charlie just runs off like that. I don't see how she has stood it this long!"

The friend continues: "I butted in and tried to explain that you would join him the minute the training period ended. But she and that Mrs. What's-Her-Name just smiled as if to say, 'What a loyal, untruthful friend you are.'" Outside of calling a town meeting and haranguing the population from the courthouse steps, I could think of no effective way to squelch the false reports; they arose each July, several weeks after Charlie had departed for training camp.

These days the rumors concerning us generally take the form of grossly exaggerated conjectures as to the amounts paid for posing for cigarette ads and writing books—harmless little gossip that tends only to bolster our credit rating.

Still another type of misconception was prevalent in those early days. While a spectator at a major golf tournament one summer, I fell to talking with a friendly young couple in the gallery (as I am wont to do). I revealed, at their request, what business my husband was in. The fellow turned to his wife and explained, matter-of-factly: "Professional football is like professional wrestling, Dear. I mean, the games are fixed." Had Jay Hebert not been bending over a tricky putt at that moment, I might have beaten the insinuator about the face and head with my folding golf seat. Similar incidents are rare today. In fact, I haven't been tempted to strike anyone for several years.

I have a final criterion for measuring the evolution of attitude toward our way of life. It concerns tone of voice. "Your husband plays PROFESSIONAL football?" has been the stock opening line of new acquaintances since our marriage in 1949. But the exclamation today bears not a trace of pity.

{3}

SIGN HERE

The contracts signed by NFL players are identical—with the exception of the figures typed on a dotted line and preceded by a dollar sign. However, it was two whole years before I discovered that the mere signing of a contract does not automatically guarantee that a player will be paid the amount stipulated! My enlightenment resulted when Charlie expressed sympathy for the fate of a halfback who had been sent home by the Giants: "I really feel sorry for that boy. He wanted to make it so badly, and I thought for awhile that he might. He surely tried hard enough." Charles shook his head. "It's really a shame he's not a little heavier. I think that's what scared them off. And of course, he was facing some stiff competition from veteran players."

Engaging in a favorite pursuit—expounding freely on subjects I know little or nothing about—I bumbled into the conversation. "I'm sorry he was released too. Such a nice fellow. I know he hates to face the folks back home, but I don't think it is as bad as you make it sound. After all, *you* have to work for twelve weeks longer to earn this year's salary. He has his in his pocket."

Charlie greeted this outburst with a look of tolerant surprise and began fumbling in a drawer. He came up with his contract. "Here. Read the fine print."

I must admit that I had never gotten further in his player-owner agreement than those interesting figures mentioned earlier. The following passage beamed loud and clear from the second page: *Should the player at any time fail to demonstrate sufficient skill and capacity to play professional football of the caliber required by the league and by the club or if in the opinion of the head coach the player's work or conduct . . . is unsatisfactory as compared with the work and conduct of the other members of the club's squad of players, the club shall have the right to terminate the contract . . .*

It was my turn to register astonishment. "Does this mean that those players who are cut from the squad *don't get paid?*"

"That's right. They don't get paid. At least not the ones who are released before the regular season starts. The team dismissing an unsuccessful candidate is required to give him only enough money to pay for his transportation home. However, I don't know about other clubs, but I do know that the Giants have been known to slip a hard-put family man a little extra cash (on the quiet) to help with the rent back home while he is finding other employment. Occasionally a player will be turned loose in the middle of the year. In that case, of course, he gets paid for those games played while he was a member of the team." Charlie went on to explain that in order to receive his contracted salary a player must first prove his ability to "make the team." A boy highly touted in college may lack the size, speed, or know-how required in professional football— where the cream of a *decade* of college crops abounds. Such a clause prevents owners from "buying a pig in a poke."

In rare instances, that paragraph is deleted from the contracts signed by players of outstanding ability. The provisional agreement is thus converted into a non-release contract. Needless to say, the holder of a "no cut" document has in some manner convinced his employer of the certainty of his worth. In most cases he is a veteran performer who has proved his value in years past and feels, as does his owner, that he has earned this measure of protection. Occasionally a rookie of indisputable quality whose services are vigorously desired in several quarters will land a non-release agreement. Such covenants are generally kept secret to avoid provoking envious thoughts among players who do not enjoy this security.

Careful reading reveals another interesting feature of the standard contract. In addition to withholding federal and state income taxes from each paycheck (as required by law), club owners are directed by league rule to hold back 25 percent of a player's total salary. This sizable check is mailed to his off-season address several days after the last game is played. Whatever the intent of this condition, it serves to protect the free-spending player from his weakness. At the season's end, an extravagant fellow might undergo a rude awakening to the fact that he has succeeded in disposing of his biweekly paycheck—biweekly! Were it not for the fact that one-fourth of his salary has been put aside *for* him, his bank balance might total zero—after five months of hard work. This enforced savings benefits also those who consider themselves reasonably conservative. It is sometimes difficult to visualize that money paid over a three-month period must, in many cases, last the whole year—and beyond.

Incidentally, the discrepancy between the five- and three-month intervals mentioned above results from the fact that a player is not paid for the two months of training which precede the three of the regular season. I should say, his *salary* does not begin until the league season starts officially. The cost of food, lodging, laundry, tips, and travel during this nine-week phase of training is assumed by the individual club. In addition, the NFL Players' Association succeeded (in 1958) in securing for each player a stopgap stipend of $50 for each exhibition game played during the training period.

An intricate network of minor league teams provides major league baseball with its principal source of fresh talent. Professional football, on the other hand, has access to hundreds of ready-made "farm teams" which require from it no organization, no supervision, no expense: every college football squad in America. After surveying the current crop of collegians considered potential pro material, officials of each National Football

League team compile a list of the graduating players they feel will best fit into their schemes of operation. Note the phrase "graduating players." The bylaws of the NFL include a commendable stipulation designed to encourage a player to complete his education before embarking on a professional career: A boy is not considered eligible for league play until his college class has been graduated. Few sports make this effort to eliminate the temptation of quitting school prematurely.

For the sake of accuracy, I should mention a rarity in professional football: the player with no college experience. During the war years, when the manpower shortage was acute, it was not unusual for a high school graduate to leap directly into the big leagues (after declaring formally that he had no intention of entering college). Today the abundance of accessible talent makes such an occurrence a phenomenon. On the fourteen 1961 team rosters, listing the more than five hundred men in the NFL, only *three* did not attend college!

At an annual meeting, coaches and owners of the fourteen NFL teams take turns in selecting players from the throng of eligible college players. The club which finished last in percentage the previous season is permitted the advantage of choosing first—and naturally claims the player considered the most valuable of the lot. Selection continues in reverse order, with the first-place team getting last pick. When each team has chosen one player, the second round begins and the third and so on until the supply of manpower has been apportioned among the fourteen teams. Each owner then sets about the business of contacting and signing his list of draftees to mutually agreeable contracts.

As mentioned earlier, Charlie signed a "mutually agreeable" five-year contract with the Giants in 1948. Since then he has negotiated on a year-to-year basis. During his career, Charlie has received a series of "mutually agreeable" raises based on one or more factors: The ever-increasing rise in the cost of living; his ever-increasing experience as a player; and on a more tangible bargaining point—performing particularly well throughout the previous season.

Actually, where Charlie is concerned, "bargaining" is something of a misnomer. For with bare exception every raise given him by Giant owners Jack and Wellington Mara was unsolicited. I remember the events of one year in particular, though essentially the same scene took place many times. Charlie was to meet Well Mara at the Senior Bowl game in Mobile for the purpose of signing his new contract. The night before he left, I was sitting on the side of the bed watching him pack. "I had a pretty good year last season," he mused. "I think I'll ask for a raise."

"You had a *wonderful* year," I amended, surreptitiously removing from the suitcase a striped tie which had always been one of my un-favorites.

"And if they don't want to give it to me, I'll just tell Well that I'll . . ." He turned his back and finished the sentence in a mumble which I couldn't decipher.

"They will," I offered. "They've always been more than fair. You know that."

"I think I deserve a raise," he said emphatically, ignoring my helpful opinion.

By the time he had slung the last bit of apparel into the suitcase (with mounting vigor), Charlie had worked out an if-he-says-that, then I'll-say-this conversation with Wellington that left him highly agitated. "Where's that striped tie I like so much?" he shouted finally.

"I think that's the one that had a spot on it. I must have sent it to the cleaners," I replied, crossing my fingers.

The following night Charlie called me from Mobile. "Did you talk to Well?" I asked finally, since he neglected to broach the subject himself.

"Yes," he said sheepishly. "And you know what happened? I went up to his room and before I even had a chance to sit down and light a cigarette, Well said, 'Charlie, you had such a good year, we think you ought to have a raise.' And he handed me a contract already filled out for the exact amount I was going to ask for—down to the last penny! So I signed it. Makes me wonder if I should have asked for more!"

I have lost count of the times the Giant offer turned out to be identical to the figure which Charlie had in mind. The whole thing got to be downright spooky. I began to wonder if they had our house bugged.

At any rate, such a meeting of minds is but one of the many reasons we think the Maras are the pleasantest of people—and by far the best bosses in the NFL.

The draft system is periodically attacked by critics as a form of "slave trading" because the player himself has no freedom of choice. He is the property of the team which drafts him, and that team has exclusive rights to his services. Despite its shortcomings, there is no other feasible method of dividing the available talent. Were the owners forced to compete on the open market for the services of prospective players, it stands to reason that the most prosperous teams in the league would be able to corral the most gifted players, and continue to do so year after year because winners draw crowds and make money. Losing teams would become weaker and weaker and finally would be forced out of business.

Actually the slave is not completely at the mercy of his master. Should he fail to come to terms with his NFL owner, there are several alternatives. He may turn to the American League team which drafted him. Or he may investigate the possibility of seeking his fortune in Canadian football. Occasionally a boy whose home is in or near a National League city is unhappy because he was drafted by a distant team and would prefer to live and work at home. Under those circumstances, most owners will make an effort to negotiate a trade which places him with the team of his choice.

The draft system is largely responsible for the surprising balance maintained among NFL teams year after year. Rarely is the title race a runaway. There are no breathers on the pro schedule. Any team is capable of defeating any other on a given day. A crucial penalty, a shoestring catch, or the absence of a key player because of injury is often the equalizer between two teams—though one may be at the top of the standings, the other at the bottom.

The telegram informing Charlie that he had been drafted by the Washington Redskins was forwarded to him on Guam in 1945. He recalls that the event made little impression on him at the time, since he was then occupied with competition of a more pressing nature. Before enlisting in the Marine Corps he had completed his sophomore year at Ole Miss. His original class was graduated two years later, thus making him eligible for the NFL draft list at that time. Charlie was discharged in January of 1946 and—under league rules—could have reported to the Redskin camp that same summer. He elected, however, to return to Ole Miss for his remaining two years of study. Meanwhile the Redskins, replete with talented passers in the form of Sammy Baugh and Harry Gilmer, traded Charlie sight unseen to the New York Football Giants. A most happy turn of events, as far as we are concerned.

Incidentally, Charlie's Pacific vacation was undoubtedly responsible for the confusion which surrounded his true age for some years afterward. Upon his return to the Ole Miss campus, compilers of the 1946 Rebel team roster took no official note of Charlie's three-year absence. They merely lifted his vital statistics from the 1942 football program and charitably added but one year to his age. Later the unsuspecting Giant publicity director adopted the conservative Ole Miss version.

Now, Charlie has never made a secret of his age. It was just that nobody ever asked him what it really was. Several years ago in a locker-room interview session, somebody did. A reporter who had written a recent article headlined: "Conerly—Amazing Old Pro at 33!" evidently intended to write a follow-up. "Charlie," he inquired, "just exactly when will you be thirty-four?"

"Been there," Charlie said casually. "I'll be thirty-six on September 19."

The gentleman of the press made a rapid calculation. "You were born in 1921!" Charlie's nod sent him scurrying out to file his scoop. Other writers subsequently pounced on the tidbit, and for weeks thereafter the number 36 (!) was emblazoned across sports pages over the country. Charlie was flabbergasted at the furor occasioned by his innocent revelation. My reaction was typically feminine: regret that I had been so free with the information that I am five and a half years younger than he. I had planned to stop counting at thirty. Now they had me pegged, too.

{4}

PRE-SEASON: THE MEN IN CAMP

Down through the years, football has become increasingly complicated, necessitating more and more study to solve the refinements of offensive and defensive maneuvers. And more and more practice to master their execution. "School" begins in July, when players report to a designated training site located, in the case of the Giants, in a cool climate. Since the camp must have an athletic field, dressing room, dormitory, and dining room facilities, the management usually chooses an off-season resort or a small college. Former training camps have been held, for example, in Wisconsin Dells and Lake Superior in Wisconsin; St. Peter, Minnesota; Hershey, Pennsylvania (where Hershey bars are made—and oh, that smell! Not so delectable before breakfast.); Willamette University in Salem, Oregon; and St. Michael's College in Winooski, Vermont. Perhaps it is no accident that the locales invariably have a small town atmosphere devoid of the distracting city influences.

Throughout the summer, prospective players receive a series of cheery little letters from the Giant front office directing them to institute individual fitness programs that will enable them to report for duty "in shape," at optimum playing weight. However, rare is the player who can discipline himself sufficiently to undertake solo workouts of the intensity desired. Despite conscientious pre-camp calisthenics at home, nearly all trainees experience a twinge of muscle soreness when the group exercises begin. Some, more than a twinge!

Team gossip has it that one gigantic tackle who has a perennial overweight problem is customarily offered by Giant owners a bonus of one thousand dollars if he checks in weighing 280 or less. He has yet to collect it. Some teams threaten to fine players fifty dollars for every pound of excess weight they bring to camp. Because of his lean, angular build Charlie has no such problem. A hometown contemporary (and friend) who fights a never-ending battle with his mushrooming waistline moans good-naturedly that "All Chaz has to do to get in shape is chew a stick of gum." Not quite true, of course, but Charlie is the only man I know of who *gains* weight in training camp. The routine whets his ordinarily meager appetite.

Players are encouraged to participate during the off-season in (non-contact) sports such as golf, tennis, handball, and the like in order to maintain stamina and keep leg muscles resilient. They are warned against an excessive amount of swimming and lolling about beaches and pools. Swimming develops muscles in the "wrong" way—to the detriment of those used most in playing football. And lolling develops *nothing* useful.

The first three weeks of this nine-week training period are the hardest. The boys lead a regimented, almost Spartan existence, as fatiguing mentally as it is physically. Field workouts are scheduled morning and afternoon, with classroom strategy meetings generously sprinkled in between. Movies are shown at night, but not for entertainment. They are football movies of last year's team in action. At the end of the day, with perhaps enough energy remaining for scribbling a letter home, our heroes fall exhausted into bed, perchance to dream of missed blocks and incompleted passes.

Invariably at this stage in the proceedings, half a dozen first-year men voluntarily turn in their shoes and head for home—some after only a day or two. Professional football is not what they thought it would be. Visions of performing before the multitudes in Yankee Stadium are overshadowed by the dull grind of work and more work, study and more study. And homesickness.

As indicated, wives are taboo at this stage. Perhaps the years have mellowed my outlook, but I now agree with the Giant brass that this initial phase of training camp is no place for family life.

Beginning with a seven-thirty breakfast, the trainees are required to show up for every meal . . . and promptly. The 11 P.M. curfew is strictly enforced. Infractions are punished by extra laps and fines. The degree of chastisement is decided by an executive committee composed of veteran players who also act as an intermediary between "labor and management" when necessary.

Charlie was a charter member of this pseudo-judicial body which came into being about six years ago. The initial meeting was enlivened by a discussion concerning the fines to be levied for various offenses. All agreed that the amounts should not be great enough to work a real hardship, yet should be substantial enough to deter repetition of the acts. A fine of twenty-five dollars was proposed as penalty for violation of the curfew, but Charlie demurred. "Not enough," he contended. "Let's make it fifty." Dissenters were outvoted, and the board accepted the higher figure.

I suppose you can guess the identity of the very first culprit apprehended in the act of entering the dormitory after hours. Correct. Old Blabbermouth himself.

"I knew I was cutting it close," Charlie explained, "but that was the best movie I've seen in years, and I just couldn't tear myself away until I saw how it ended."

He consoled himself with the thought that the fifty was not a total loss, since the fines assessed in training camp are used to finance a party for all the players and their wives at the end of the season. I don't know whether the boys these days are better, or the movies worse—but lack of funds in recent years has necessitated going Dutch treat to our annual team soiree.

Each year approximately sixty players report to try out for the team. Only thirty-six will make it. Unfortunately, talent and desire are not the only factors which determine whether or not a candidate is successful in his bid to break into the big leagues. Luck plays a major role.

The prime consideration in a coach's selection of the final squad is need—the need for men who play certain positions. Take, for the sake of illustration, two mythical players who man entirely different positions, a tackle and a defensive halfback. Imagine that the tackle is reporting to a team which includes on its roster five veteran tackles—not to mention several "hot college prospects" in addition to himself. He may find his chances slight, since that team customarily employs only five tackles.

On the other hand, suppose the backfield man is fortunate to find the competition in the defensive halfback division not so keen. Consequently, he may be snapped up to fill the gap caused by a predecessor's retirement, injury, or absence because of military service. Though halfback and tackle are equally talented, one fills a definite need. The other does not. It is simply a matter of timing. Another year the situation could be reversed. (In any case, despair not. If our make-believe tackle is good enough, he will be picked up by a club that is shorthanded in the tackle department.)

Since a winning team will, if possible, be kept more or less intact the following year, many first-year men are victims of this don't-tamper-with-success theory. Having won the world championship in 1956, the Giants deemed it necessary to fill only three vacancies in 1957. Of the thirty-two eager rookies in camp only *two* were selected. (The third opening was manned via a trade.) I do not mean to imply that it is impossible for a rookie to oust an established player from any given position. It happens frequently. But all other things being equal, experience will tip the scale in favor of the veteran.

A man who plays on a team one year is not guaranteed a job the next. As I noted, each player's contract states that he must at all times meet the standards of a pro player as decided by his coach. He must make the team and keep on making it—not only from year to year, but from game to game. With this in mind it might be interesting to take a closer look at the pre-season exhibition games, which are generally dismissed lightly by the sports public for three reasons:

1. Because of extensive experimentation, the brand of football is sometimes below par.
2. The games don't "count" in the league standings.
3. Therefore the boys don't try.

The first two assumptions are true. The latter could not be farther from the truth. Indeed these practice games furnish a coach the opportunity of transferring new theories from the blackboard to the field of action and of tuning up the old reliable strategies. This is also the time for evaluating untried personnel. Sloppy execution sometimes results from this combination of trials. However, the exhibition games are played while the roster still bulges with hopefuls, who know but few of their number will make the grade. They know the coaches are watching every move they make. They know that no matter how promising a prospect appears in practice, he must be able to produce under fire to be of value. They know that performance in those games may draw the fine line between those who make it and those who will soon be seeking employment elsewhere.

You might conclude (and correctly) that what the games lack in finesse, they make up in spirited individual effort. The next time you have the opportunity to see a pre-season contest, watch that rookie halfback dig for extra yardage. Then study his veteran counterpart in rebuttal. The older pro also runs with a vengeance—as if somebody is trying to take his job away from him. Somebody is.

An applicant accustomed to special consideration in local circles because of his designation as an "All-American" will be in for a rude shock if he expects these niceties to continue in his present surroundings. Such honors are the rule, rather than the exception, among his fellow pros.

Seasoned players generally adopt a wait-and-see attitude toward novices. A new arrival must first prove himself as a performer and as a man before the average veteran will bother getting to know him as a person. "Can he take it as well as dish it out?" they want to know. A casual observer of the training camp scene might interpret the prevailing aloofness toward first-year men as an attitude of disparagement, or even mild antagonism. However, the emotions involved are not nearly so intense and could be described more accurately as natural indifference. The fierce spirit of competition certainly exists but is usually left on the field.

The returning player simply has more in common, age-wise and otherwise, with other veterans. Much in the manner of a salesman attending an annual hardware convention in Chicago, he seeks out old friends first. Then if he finds time for an especially pleasant new acquaintance, fine. If not—*so?* (as we say in the Bronx). The mortality rate of rookies is so high that cultivating the friendship of a beginner is often effort wasted. Chances are he will fail to show up for breakfast one morning because he is presently aboard a plane bound for his home in Keokuk, having been released the night before. (For this reason it is generally unwise to accept IOUs in a pinochle game.) The enervating routine also tends to curtail the customary social amenities. And, as a perennial Giant once summed up the rookie situation: "There are just so damn *many* of them!"

This apparent conspiracy of cold-shoulder-ism received widespread newspaper coverage a few years back because of the "treatment" given rookie quarterback Lee Grosscup. During a visit to New York undertaken for the purpose of signing his Giant contract, Lee not only met his future teammates, but also made the acquaintance of a personable newspaperman, with whom he subsequently corresponded from December to July. A few weeks before reporting to training camp, Lee was contacted by the writer who asked permission to publish his letters in a national magazine in order to exemplify the hopes and fears of a boy entering pro football. Lee had always harbored a desire to become a journalist, and recalling nothing offensive in what he had written, agreed.

Unfortunately, in the cold light of print the letters lost much of their intended lightheartedness. His opinions of pro football and his impressions of his teammates-to-be were considered silly by some Giant players and downright annoying by others. Newsmen, smelling a human interest story, converged on the training camp as soon as the article appeared and found what they were seeking. Lee was a loner—an outcast, spoken to only by other rookies.

What they failed to note was that rookies of far less notoriety were also doing a lot of talking to each other—in the absence of insistent invitations to converse with their "elders." I can't say the controversial article made no difference. I'm sure it did. I do contend that the prevailing attitude toward Lee that summer was one of pity rather than antagonism. Rare is the novice who charms his way into the "inner circle" instantly, and chances are, Lee would not have had the opportunity, article or no article.

I must admit that I was anxious to meet the "author." I found him darkly handsome, pleasant, rather quiet, and young. (His mother is a year younger than Charlie!)

Lee's problem prompted me to ask Charlie just who *his* friends were when he was a rookie. "That's been a long time ago," he replied, "but I recall spending most of my time with Ray Poole and Joe Johnson." Ray was a second-year man and Joe was a rookie. Both had been teammates of Charlie's at Ole Miss.

Most of the players in camp are under provisional contract. However, a few "free agents," overlooked in the draft selection, join the group—hoping to impress the coaches with performance in lieu of reputation. Few are successful. However, the Giants once lucked up on a pretty fair football player in this manner, name of Emlen Tunnel. For eleven years Em terrorized Giant opponents with his defensive deftness (interceptions, a specialty); he then continued his amazing career in a Packer uniform.

After three weeks of grueling routine the pre-season exhibition games begin, and the monotony is relieved somewhat as the team breaks camp and takes to the road. Practice sessions abate to one a day. Scrimmages are fewer. The squad becomes smaller and smaller as the inept, unwilling, unneeded, and lazy are systematically weeded out. Emotional strain heightens. Imagine the inner turmoil of a boy who wonders, as his less fortunate mates fall by the wayside, if he will be one of the final thirty-six.

I might add that the coaches dread the cutting season almost as much as the hapless players do. The head coach informs unsuccessful candidates that their services are no longer required. "It is no easy task," former Giant coach Jim Lee Howell once said, "to hand a man such a blow to his pride—and to his pocketbook. The loss of anticipated income is bad enough, but the embarrassment of admitting to the home folks that he was not good enough is possibly worse."

Were wives encouraged to become "camp followers," few could afford the expense of traveling from one end of the country to another. However, those fortunate enough to live in or near the cities where the five or six exhibition games are played (or where the latter-phase encampments are located) are permitted to join their husbands for brief pre-season rendezvous.

Since the team ordinarily sets up housekeeping near New York City during the final weeks of training (Bear Mountain Inn, New York, or Fairfield University, Connecticut), I customarily jump the gun by several weeks. Texans Kyle and Betty Rote now live permanently in Scarsdale, New York. Using the Rote home as headquarters, I pay periodic visits to Charles at the nearby training site. Between trips, Betty and I frequently outlast the Late Late Show while catching each other up on the between-season happenings. Gossip is what it is.

{5}

THE WIVES ARRIVE

The start of the regular league season (the latter part of September) is an event met with diverse emotions in various quarters throughout the nation. The prevailing attitudes range from anti-pro to violently pro-pro. The football fanatic, for instance, is ecstatic at the thought of fourteen consecutive Sundays filled with exciting gridiron action, not to mention the championship game and various other post-season contests.

His wife, on the other hand, may not be so thrilled—particularly if her interest in the game is limited, and her taste runs instead to family visits or to movies. She may be horrified to find the master of the house suddenly transformed from a thoughtful husband and father into a silent, entranced TV-watcher who lashes out at the slightest disturbance created by his wife and their adorable children while The Game is in progress.

Between those extremes there is, I'm told, a segment of the population on whom the opening game makes no impression at all. These people simply don't care one way or the other. Such outright apathy is inconceivable to me. But in all fairness I must be charitable. Peering through binoculars at a pair of ruby-throated humming-birds at play has never especially interested *me*; after all, it is not to my credit that the only birds I care to watch are the Eagles and the Cardinals.

Two remaining groups feel quite strongly on the subject. One is composed of the wives of professional football coaches. The coaches' ladies I have known greet each new season with a feeling of dread—or pretend to, anyhow. "When the games begin I might as well move out and leave home for three months," one harried coach's wife told me. "And if it weren't for the fact that my husband would then surely give up eating and sleeping *completely*, I might."

"I know that half the time I am talking to him," said another, "his mind is on the fifty-yard line instead of on the new suit for Jimmie I've just mentioned. He looks right through me sometimes. I also have the feeling that when he *is* fully conscious, he is taking his disappoint-ment in the rookie halfback out on my pot roast. Such a grouch! And to think, off-season he has the best disposi-tion of any man I know.

"Just when I think I have talked him into a quiet evening of family conversation or television, he suddenly leaps up from the supper-table shouting, 'I know why that 28 Slant didn't work against Cleveland!' He proceeds to set up the movie projector in the living room and then runs the same film over and over—squinting and mutter-ing to himself far into the night. I try to be sympathetic because I know the pressure is terrible, but the next time he draws a 28 Slant on my best damask tablecloth (then swears he doesn't remember doing it), I plan to dent his skull (only slightly) with his prized college trophy!"

"I have actually developed a small ulcer," a coach's wife confided, "and that being the case, I'm sure 'The Coach' must have one the size of a regulation football. But he doesn't 'have time' to see a doctor!"

Still another band of individuals whose lives are altered annually by the start of the league season welcomes the event: pro football players and their families. The next three months will bring them worry, disappointment—perhaps even fear. But these disagreeable aspects are overshadowed by the numerous attractive features of "playing for keeps." Each team returns to its home city, and the peripatetic existence of the past weeks is gratefully exchanged for an interval of comparative normalcy. In 1957—after thirty-two years of tedious train trips to out-of-town games—the Giant management gave in to the expediency of plane travel. Consequently, during the season, players need be absent from the city only one night every other week.

Wives and children arrive, and unpleasant memories of training camp fade away amidst the joys of reunion, home-fried chicken, and clean socks every day.

The pro player counts still more blessings engendered by the start of the league season. First and foremost of these are the physical demands of the regular season. Though by no means meager, they are considered almost trivial when compared to the rigors of training camp. His state of mind improves. The repetitious procedures necessary to attain facility of execution suddenly take on meaning. He is now confronted with an exciting series of individual goals (each game) which points to the ultimate goal (the league championship).

In addition, a Giant player is permitted to live anywhere in the New York area he pleases. He begins receiving a biweekly paycheck—a welcome change in financial weather after the long drought. He may formulate his own schedule, so long as it includes reporting for the daily practice sessions and showing up for the games on Sunday. There is no longer a fixed curfew. However, he is now what that TV commercial would call a "mature male" and realizes that lethargic performance caused by late hours will eventually jeopardize his job. Even the so-called good timers in the league curtail such extracurricular activities as the weekend approaches. No intelligent businessman would run the risk of botching up a million-dollar deal by arriving at a vital conference with his mind befogged (unless, perhaps, his father owns the company). The pro football player is a businessman who must consider the state of his body as well. (And I don't know of a single pro player who calls his boss Dad.)

Those short on self-discipline seldom require an official reprimand from coaches or owners for questionable conduct. Disapproval expressed or implied by their teammates is likely to make offenders aware that the thirty-six players on a team are interdependent. "None of my business?" I heard one disgruntled player say of the antics of a teammate. "That's a laugh! He *is* my business. If we lost a game because he fell asleep during skull practice, brother, that's money out of my pocket!"

Several days before the boys are scheduled to arrive in New York for the start of the league season, I move into our apartment in the Concourse Plaza Hotel to begin the chore of unpacking the boxes sent from home and of prowling the musty storage closets in search of more boxes containing an ever-increasing accumulation of duplicated household necessities. Kitchen utensils, for example, would be rather bulky to ship back and forth, so I have a makeshift collection which the hotel keeps for me. Before leaving New York each year, I dutifully mark the boxes with the name of a player who is planning to return for another year of play (because Charlie swears each year *he* is *not*) and include instructions to dole out the contents among the rookie wives—a wasted precaution thus far. After seeking out the other early-arriving wives and exchanging greetings, I stock up on groceries and flip through the cookbook to refresh my memory. (I become very friendly with the can opener during Charlie's prolonged absences.)

We choose this hotel for our on-season home because it is three short blocks from Yankee Stadium, where the boys play on Sunday and practice daily during the week. The hotel claims to be the "business and social center of the Bronx." As far as I know, it is the *only* hotel in the Bronx. But a very nice one at that. Charlie and I feel quite at home after thirteen seasons there.

There is a shopping center nearby, and both East and West Side subways are only a block away. It takes but twenty minutes to reach Times Square—a distance of some 120 blocks. There is a park across the street where the children may be taken in good weather to expend excess energy. Generally the team fathers are tapped to escort the sandpile set to the park and supervise their play. Perhaps Mom contends that she deserves a few minutes of solitude after being confined in a hotel apartment with several lively youngsters all morning. Or perhaps their family includes an infant too young for the great outdoors, with whom she must remain at home. At any rate, the fathers usually contact other fathers—in order to insure adult companionship during the baby-sitting stints—and the group sets out for the park in a body. It is an appealing sight to watch these rugged and fierce men tenderly buttoning tiny coats and blowing tiny noses.

Before the Giffords and Rotes moved to the suburbs, their two oldest boys (along with young Tom Landry, whose dad now coaches the Dallas Cowboys) were the hub of a neighborhood football game in the park. Play began after school each day and continued until almost dark. I have a feeling that names like Gifford, Rote, and Landry didn't hinder the boys' chances of getting to play their favorite positions. In bad weather young Kyle and Tom would sit by the hour and draw plays which were amazingly workable. (Jeff Gifford was then a few months too young to be of much help in these strategy conferences.)

One season the twelve Giant couples who lived at the Concourse Plaza boasted a total of twenty children. However, school is a problem for only a few team parents because a player's career usually ends before his children are old enough to go. (The current official survey shows that the average length of service for an NFL player is 4.25 years.) School-age children in the hotel are customarily sent to private schools recommended by the team's owners.

Although the amount of rent we pay in New York seems astronomical when compared with lease prices in Clarksdale, we console ourselves with the fact that "It is only for three months." During our first few seasons in the city, I looked for (and found) numerous apartments which would have cost less. Unlike those in our hotel, they were either unfurnished and/or required the signing of a year-round lease—making them impractical for our use for both reasons. Besides, the dormitory atmosphere which prevails in the Concourse is not only fun, but a great comfort when the boys are out of town or out making banquet speeches at night.

On Long Island and in Westchester, among other places distant to the Stadium, there are apartment hotels which offer more space for less money than we pay. However, the cost and strain of commuting and the extra hour's sleep we would lose by living there make up the difference as far as Charlie and I are concerned.

A number of the New York Yankees live in the Concourse Plaza during the baseball season, and their winning habits traditionally cause our group a certain amount of inconvenience. No one pulls harder for a four-game World Series than those among us who were late in making reservations. For during the overlap in seasons these unfortunates must languish in single rooms while waiting for the Yankees to vacate the remaining apartments. (The annoyance is lessened by the fact that most of us are Yankee fans.)

The Giants as a team also find the perennial good fortune of the Yankees a mite troublesome. Until the World Series ends, football practice sessions are held forty blocks away at Fordham University instead of at the Stadium. Before last season (when a building program was completed at the school) certain of the athletic facilities left something to be desired. I remember assistant coach Harlan Svare's description of the former defensive meeting place: "Well, it's a powder room. It really is. There are sixteen of us crammed in there sitting bumper to bumper on those little folding chairs—the kind they used to have at Sunday school. I shudder every time I see Rosie Grier's three hundred pounds on that little pile of kindling. You should see us when Jim [former coach Jim Lee Howell] comes in to meet with us. We all have to stand up and fold up our chairs to make room for him to walk in. Then when he gets seated, there's a mad rush to unfold because the last three don't get to. They have to stand and hold their chairs until he leaves. It's a real circus!"

Several of the unmarried players live in downtown hotels, but none that I know of has access to a kitchen, a requirement for family living. Sometimes two or three of the single boys or those classed as temporary bachelors (because their wives found it necessary to remain at home) pool their resources and share an apartment in the hotel. What a sight it was to see roommates Don Boll (6' 2½", 285 lb.) and Frank Youso (6' 4", 265 lb.) squeezing the tomatoes in the local supermarket and planning the week's menu as they strolled among the other shopping "housewives." Pity the poor butcher who gets caught trying to give those two a short weight!

Some players live the year round in the city of play. Of these, a few are natives of the area. Others have moved there since entering pro football in order to take advantage of off-season business opportunities. However, the majority of players are faced with the problem of finding suitable living quarters for their temporarily transplanted families. Nearly all move their families up, though some wives remain behind for various reasons—advanced pregnancy being the most common deterrent.

Squeals of joy ring throughout the corridors of the Concourse Plaza as arriving wives are greeted in turn by their predecessors, who have been alerted through the efficiency of the hotel grapevine. From twenty states they come. But geography poses no barrier to friendship. Accents vary, but the language of the football wife is universal. Although currently only 25 percent of the team is composed of Southerners, in years past the proportion has ranged as high as 50 percent. Relatives of California or Ohio wives are understandably perplexed when the girls return home from New York, their speech marked by a definite trace of Southern accent!

Though it is better to give than to receive, close association with our cosmopolitan group has resulted in certain linguistic concessions on my part. While in New York, I pronounce the "r" in Conerly, especially when identifying myself over the phone. I say "dinner" when I really mean "supper." And I say "Pardon?" when I fail to understand what someone says. Once back home, I have no difficulty in dropping the "r" or in saying "supper" when I mean supper; but I sometimes unconsciously revert to the use of "Pardon?" an unfamiliar idiom where I live. Constantly chided about this lapse, I contend adamantly that it is simpler than "What did you say?" and more refined than "Huh?"

Several days after the gathering of the clan—allowing time for the business of setting up temporary housekeeping—I customarily invite the hotel wives and children for a get-acquainted coffee and cookie session. And what hectic affairs. Fifteen women and twenty children in one small apartment. Though the lively antics of the little people invariably result in several minor casualties, fortunately no fatalities have been recorded. The Bravest-Soul-of-All Award (All-Time Team Record) goes to petite Pattie Shaw, wife of quarterback George. Pattie arrived smilingly at the 1959 welcome-back party with a child under each arm and a third clinging to her coattail. The oldest was two and a half at the time.

It is fun for all of us to note the changes in the team children from one year to the next. During the nine-month interval the two-year-olds invariably graduate from hair-pulling to biting. ("I can't imagine where she learned *that!*") The three-year-olds, formerly a group of irrepressible chatterboxes, become shy and mute. The four-year-olds learn to shake hands and to tell their ages—*without* fingers!

The wives change too. Innovations wrought by last year's off-season featured three new babies and four new blondes! It is perhaps a philosophical commentary on womankind that the daring exhibited by the four former brunettes occasioned almost as much delight as did the genetic accomplishments of the three new mothers.

It may be interesting to note that most football players marry either hometown girls or college sweethearts. In my thirteen years as a pro I can recall only three Giants who met their future wives during the season.

I may be slightly prejudiced, but Giant wives (in fact, football wives in general) are as charming and attractive a group of young ladies as can be found anywhere. And I must admit I get a tiny bit irritated when people who meet them act *too* surprised to find them so. One must assume that such a reaction (though complimentary in intent) implies dismal expectations. Through long-time friends, Charlie and I once met a city-bred couple who were mutually positive that the civilized world ended at the New Jersey state line. I sat next to the husband during dinner that night. Our small talk was punctuated by his florid praise of the dress I was wearing. At first I was flattered, but he kept on and on, the note of incredulity in his voice growing stronger with each compliment. Finally he said, "I just can't get over it. You look so nice. And your husband's a football player. On top of that you're from Mississippi!"

Anxious to change the subject, for once and all, I finally said: "We get the mail-order catalogue down there too." That should have done the job—except that he took me seriously and berated his wife throughout the evening for her needless extravagance in buying clothes at Saks!

{6}

NEW YORK IS A WINTER FESTIVAL

Certainly much of the enormous pleasure Charlie and I have derived from pro football stems from the fact that the "home office" is located in the most exciting city in the world. Perhaps our lengthy stay would have been just as enjoyable had we been assigned to another NFL city. I cannot attest to the glamour of Green Bay or Pittsburgh, for example; but I rather doubt that either can equal New York in that category.

Both Charlie and I were born in Clarksdale, Mississippi; the "Golden Buckle on the Cotton Belt" is our home and always will be considered as such, no matter where the future leads us. Indeed, there's no place like home (she sang softly), but our three-and-a-half-month stay in the big city provides a pleasant change of pace for us. We have succeeded rather well, I think, in taking advantage of the outstanding diversions it offers.

After spending over a decade of autumns there, we claim New York as our second hometown, and I beam with civic pride while showing it off to visiting friends. I have become a passable guide these last thirteen years, for I stand ready to conduct either a thorough week-long tour of the city or my special whirlwind outing, designed for those who can devote only one day to seeing the sights. I never tire of these excursions, but I must admit that the number of sightseeing trips undertaken exclusively for my personal benefit has dropped off sharply in the past few years.

There was a time, however, when I was the most enthusiastic, appreciative, and persistent tourist in Greater New York. Museums, churches, art galleries, department stores, zoos, Wall Street, Fifth Avenue, Coney Island, Rockefeller Center, Greenwich Village, the Empire State Building, the Statue of Liberty (still my favorite) . . . I ogled everything I had ever heard about—even Grant's Tomb!

Charles was constantly amazed at the daily report of my wanderings. In the first place, with no natural sense of direction, I had been notoriously timid about venturing into unfamiliar territory unaccompanied. In fact, until that time (1949), the largest city with which I was reasonably well acquainted was Memphis, Tennessee. Since Memphis is located only seventy miles north of Clarksdale, I had been there hundreds of times; but Charlie knew I was unable to go around the block without getting lost at least once. My new-found independence baffled him.

Frequent expeditions into various sections of Manhattan gradually increased my self-reliance. I overcame a misfiring sense of direction with a bit of street corner weathervaning—an elemental system of pathfinding based on the happy discovery that the streets in New York are numbered so logically. (Forty-second Street is between Forty-first and Forty-third, for example, with the higher-numbered streets to the north.) I found the avenues also reasonably predictable with the exception of Broadway, which meanders about at will.

Before long I was on a first-name basis with the subway. I learned the little tricks that come from vast experience:

- Unless the northbound "D" is against the wall at 145th, step off and catch a local—or you roar past Yankee Stadium and into the hinterlands.
- Never *rise* to offer your seat to an old lady. Ask her *before* you relinquish it—or the man standing at her elbow will plop down while she is recovering from the shock of your offer.
- When patted or pinched by a rush-hour masher, frown fiercely and shout loudly, "All right! Cut it out or I'll call the trainman!" The fondler may be so startled by your outburst that he will desist, temporarily forgetting two facts:
  1. Because the train is so jammed you have no idea which of the innocent-looking men in your vicinity is the culprit.
  2. A slippery midget could not penetrate the mass of humanity to come to your aid—much less a hefty trainman.

Occasionally these affectionate souls risk positive identification on not-so-crowded trains. I once held a fanny-feeler at bay for eighty blocks by brandishing a tightly-clenched umbrella just above his bald pate. During that time neither of us spoke a word. Instead, I mustered a menacing scowl—which was, unfortunately, in constant danger of bursting into an amused giggle. For the little old man seemed completely oblivious to the fact that we were frozen in a tableau that might have been titled "Injured Innocence." I, sullen and threatening, with my weapon poised to strike at the slightest false move; he wearing the most cherubic expression seen in public since Shirley Temple was six!

The subway has afforded me many interesting, less trying hours. Most passengers read to while away the time, but I have never been able to master the art of folding and refolding a newspaper until it is the size of a playing card (a trick necessitated by the crowded conditions). Instead I study my fellow travelers, classifying them as to occupation, disposition, and circumstances. I mentally catalogue the butchers who are mad at their wives, the wives who are mad at their butchers, and so on. It is a fascinating game.

When I solo in a taxi, I cannot resist making city-wise comments: "Take the Drive, please," or, "Through the Park"—so that the driver will not mistake me for some kind of hick because of my accent. Actually this attempt at being classed as a New Yorker has another motive: Most cabbies would otherwise enumerate points of interest

I have seen a hundred times before. Invariably, when such a ride is over, they turn and ask why I chose to spend my vacation in an out-of-the-way place like the Bronx, adding that many of the ballplayers stay at the same hotel. The only answer I can ever think of is the truth—which makes both of us feel a trifle uncomfortable after his well-meant, but wasted spiel.

In 1949, my freshman year in New York, only a handful of Giant wives lived at the Concourse Plaza. Fortunately, among them was another newlywed with a penchant for adventure, Joanne (Mrs. Carl) Fennema from Seattle. She quickly joined my See-and-Do Club. When rainy weather made sightseeing impractical, often the two of us would cross the street to the Bronx County Courthouse and roam the halls until we happened on an interesting divorce case in progress. Occasionally we would luck into a murder trial.

Joanne and I saw literally every play on Broadway that season, for matinee tickets were priced as low as $1.20. We didn't mind sitting in the balcony since most of the theatres are approximately the size of the Clarksdale High School Auditorium, and even the last row affords a reasonable view of the stage.

It was during this era that conventioneers were pleading for the privilege of paying a hundred dollars for a pair of tickets to *South Pacific*. Joanne, an enterprising sort, routed me out of bed early one morning and we rushed down to stand in the *South Pacific* standing-room line. (At that time standee tickets to hit shows were not sold in advance, but put on sale daily on a first-come, first-served basis.) We arrived two hours before the box office was scheduled to open and took our places in a queue that already stretched almost to the corner. It was bitterly cold that day, and the light rain that began to fall sent a chill up my Mississippi spine. My friend from the Great Northwest was undaunted, noticing only that the line had begun to advance. Finally a little man counting out loud approached and said, "Sorry folks. No more after *these* two," indicating Joanne and me. We were in!

My fatigue vanished when the curtain went up. I was so entranced I do believe the time would have passed just as quickly had I been standing on my head. And all for $1.20!

As it turned out, each group of Clarksdalians who visited us during the next few years had *South Pacific* on its must list. I enjoyed it as much the fifth time as the first. The third time around Charlie and I were guests of a friend on an expense account and were amazed to discover (from the second row) that Pinza had a mustache!

Living in New York also provides the opportunity for indulging in another favorite hobby—eating. I would like to sample every restaurant in the city (well, *almost* every restaurant), but the guide book reports that there are over 20,000. One for every man, woman, and child in Clarksdale! Though we experiment from time to time seeking variety of menu, we are drawn to several establishments in particular: Toots Shor's, Mike Manuche's, P. J. Clarke's, Eddie Condon's, Downey's, and "21." Perhaps it is not coincidence that the managements of our favorite restaurants are extremely sports-conscious, and welcome with a broad show of recognition not only the players but also their wives.

It is a sports-conscious town. Athletes in general are interested in and well-informed about all sports—not merely the one in which they participate. Whenever I linger on the fringe of a casual conversation among Giant players, the topic is rarely professional football. More likely it centers around Arnold Palmer's hot round in a recent golf tournament, Whitey Ford's outstanding season in 1961, the Mantle-Maris home run race, Bob Cousy's continuing prowess with a basketball, the week's upset in college football, and so on.

In support of the mutual-interest theory I remember reading in 1960 that, on completing a World Series game one Sunday, the bulk of the Yankee team rushed from the field and crowded around the locker room television set. They arrived just in time to see a sore-armed quarterback named C. Conerly come off the bench and toss a field-spanning pass to Frank Gifford, who galloped in for the score that defeated the Pittsburgh Steelers in the waning seconds. Writers on the scene reported that this improbable feat generated more outward excitement among the baseball players than winning their own game had.

Since the city of New York is one big sports arena,* Giant players (and wives) are able to attend many of the

---

*I hereby take a solemn pledge that this chapter was neither suggested nor subsidized by the New York City Chamber of Commerce.

events we enjoy reading about. Both Charlie and I, loyal to the home front, cheer vociferously for the New York Yankees, Knicks, Rangers—yes, even the Titans.

The regular baseball season is just about spent when we arrive on the scene, but we manage to see at least one World Series game each year—if the Yankees win the pennant. This hardly deserves mention since the Yankees have missed only two series in the last thirteen years. Even if I weren't interested in baseball, I would make a concerted effort to attend the World Series. I am an inveterate bargain hunter. People come thousands of miles and spend hundreds of dollars to attend the classic. You can't help thinking of all the money you save by merely strolling three short blocks to the Stadium!

The game I remember most vividly is one I almost saw, but didn't. We had tickets for the fifth game that year, but Brooklyn won the first two handily. I became uncomfortably aware of the fact that a four-game sweep would leave us with a pair of colorful bookmarks. Going through the lobby the next day, I chanced on the opportunity of buying a ticket to the third game—but the Giants had left that morning on a road trip. Subduing several sharp pangs of guilt, I rationalized: "Charlie certainly wouldn't want you to risk missing the Series altogether just because *he* can't go to today's game, too." I went. The morning of the fifth game arrived (my misgivings were unfounded, for the Yankees took games three and four). I really wanted to go, but my conservative streak came to the fore. After all, Series tickets aren't cheap, and I *had* seen one game already. Suddenly I saw a chance to appear self-sacrificing and save $12.50 at the same time. Don Heinrich had never seen a World Series and wanted to go *so* badly. "Take my ticket to Don," I offered bravely.

The year was 1956. The date was October 8. While another Don (named Larsen) pitched the historic perfect game, I squirmed in front of the television set, periodically popping myself on the forehead with the heel of my hand and muttering to Mel Allen (who didn't seem to be listening): "I could have *been* there! I could have seen it with my *own eyes!*"

When Heinrich and Charlie burst into the apartment, grinning broadly, I was the first to speak. By this time, charity and compassion had vanished. "Oh, shut up!" I said.

We attend several basketball games at Madison Square Garden each year and an occasional hockey game (the most notable to be detailed later). Charlie is also a fight fan and goes whenever the opportunity presents itself. After years of watching at least two fights a week on television with him, I finally persuaded him to take me along to a "live" one. The first thing that struck me was the fact that (unlike the television version) it was all in color! The trunks were *purple* and the blood was *red*. The second thing that struck me was a splatter of the latter— all over my new suit (we had very good seats). This gory baptism, coupled with a fingernail-on-blackboard aversion to the eerie snorts and grunts being emitted by the fighters only three feet away, persuaded me to regain my armchair status.

Actually our weekly schedule seldom contains more than one special event (apart from our regular Sunday and Monday night outings). I like to cook (the outgrowth of a hobby mentioned earlier), and a typical evening includes dinner at home followed by television.

Charlie frequently does homework at night. He studies his playbook for a while, then decorates a shirt cardboard or two with those mysterious Xs and Os in order to fix them firmly in his mind. The playbook is always guarded with a caution commensurate to the five hundred dollar fine a player must pay if he loses it.

Couples in the hotel often get together for an evening of bridge or Scrabble or just conversation. Sometimes they pool their resources for a two- or three-family dinner.

In days gone by, Charles and I occasionally challenged the Rotes to a game of bridge. But Mr. C. is the restless type, and after each stint as dummy had to be summoned from behind a newspaper or a book to continue the play. I finally gave up on him.

Betty Rote keeps Charlie supplied with best sellers during the season. On meeting for the first time following the off-season interlude, Kyle and I greet each other warmly with a hug and a smack. Not Charles and Betty. No hellos for them. Just, "Let's see what you have there." And each rushes to check the other's summer collection of paperbacks.

Because I keep a scrapbook, I've never been able to sit down to watch television without a pair of scissors in my hand. Charlie goes out for newspapers several times a day, and I cannot bring myself to throw away a single one until I have checked the sports page carefully for mention of his name. There is something slightly irreverent about mutilating a newspaper on the very day it comes out. Instead of clipping the pertinent article the minute I decide it is worth saving, I lay the paper aside, thinking: "Later—when you're not so—well—*virginal.*" And so they accumulate at the rate of about forty-five a week forcing me to peruse and discard somewhere close to that amount each week.

During the month preceding Charlie Conerly Day in 1959, the atmosphere around our household was rather hectic. When that thrilling event came and went and I finally floated back down to the Real World, newspapers were leering at me from every corner of the apartment! Hundreds and hundreds of newspapers—in the chairs, under the beds, in the closet, piled behind the draperies . . . they were winning, and they seemed to know it.

Remember the tale of the hungry little girl who wished for a magic porridge pot that would never be empty? Her wish came true; and no matter how much porridge was dipped from this marvelous kettle, twice that much miraculously appeared. Soon the stuff spilled out of the cottage where she lived. Before long the streets were running with porridge, and the townspeople had to flee for their lives.

The stacks of newspapers had me feeling like a Porridgeville invalid who had been left behind in the rush for the hills. In moments of weakness I entertained the thought of tossing a match and stepping back. Sanity prevailed, however. I had newsprint from my eyebrows to my elbows every night for weeks. (Why do New York papers "shed" so much worse than others?) But at last I slew the monster.

Occasionally we vary the routine by having guests in for dinner. Sometimes these events are worth writing home about. For several years Charlie and I have been quite friendly with Faye Emerson. One night as we were having dinner with Faye and her escort at a downtown restaurant, her entree (very French and very elegant) arrived. Faye sighed wistfully. "You know I'm a Texas girl," she said, "and what I wouldn't give for a real Southern dinner. It's been so long!"

In the same breath Charlie and I invited Faye for supper the following week. I complied with the whole bit: fried chicken, rice and gravy, black-eyed peas, okra, squash and onions, and cornbread.

Some weeks earlier I asked the local supermarket man to order frozen peas and okra. The manager had heard of black-eyed peas, but couldn't imagine *why* I wanted them. As for okra: "How do you spell it? What is it?" he wanted to know. His eyes narrowed in disbelief when I told him it was a green vegetable. He was still muttering to himself as I left the office.

Naturally I was a little pessimistic about the outcome, but behold! About two weeks later I noticed the store freezer was positively overflowing with both. Consequently, I frantically touted the Southern families in the hotel to buy plenty of each so the trusting soul wouldn't be stuck with them. I even tried converting Northerners and Middle Westerners. The Conerlys did their share to deplete the inventory, but as sales increased, so did the supply. Finally Charles moaned, "Hey, I like both peas and okra very much, but *this* is ridiculous. For heaven's sake, let's have some cabbage or spinach or something for a change!" He detests both, so I bowed to the wishes of my breadwinner and left the bewildered store manager to flounder in a sea of Southern delicacies. I wonder if he was reminded of the story of the magic bowl of porridge?

MID-WORD

On occasion I have been asked by people exhibiting more curiosity than tact, "What makes *you* qualified to write about football?" Always the optimist, I assume that what they really mean is, "How did you get interested in the game?" or "Did you know anything about football before Charlie?" Anyway, I reply on that basis and begin by pointing out that (through necessity) I write not so much about the intricacies of the game itself as about the men who play it—concentrating on the inside story. I liken myself to the broadcaster who contributes the "color" portion of the show, rather than the play-by-play account.

Then, if my inquisitor remains sufficiently attentive, I launch into a bit of family history, to wit: Since I was the third of three girls, and it seemed the Collier family would have no male heir, I was Daddy's little boy. He taught me to spin a top, shoot marbles, crack a bullwhip, throw a baseball ("Snap your wrist. You're throwing like a *girl!*"), chin myself from the lower limb of the pecan tree, row a boat, and various other useful skills.

Beginning when I was eight years old or thereabouts, each Saturday afternoon during the fall Daddy would take a shirt cardboard and mark off the diagram of a football field. Then as we listened to the radio account of the college games, he would have me move a pin along to simulate the position of the ball—all the while supplementing the announcer's explanation with elemental pointers of his own. Previously, while attending the local high school games, my attention had rested primarily with the goodies available at the hot dog stand. Through Daddy's persistent instruction, I gradually became interested in the action on the field—which might have been the whole idea after all, now that I think about it!

It was only natural that I developed into something of a tomboy. Daddy always made sure I owned a softball and bat ("They'll *have* to let you play if you furnish the equipment."), though both he and Mother were somewhat less enthusiastic about my prowess as a halfback. I was never allowed to own a football. Nevertheless, I almost always managed to win a spot on the neighborhood team whenever I was able to elude Mother. She recalls with a slight shudder (even after all these years) the time I was scheduled to represent "Mistress Summer" in a junior high pageant. On the morning of the program she was obliged to sew streamers down one side of my costume to conceal a fearsome thigh abrasion incurred the previous afternoon when I had been clotheslined on an end run and skidded for several yards in a section of the playing field that was singularly devoid of grass.

Fortunately, as time went by, my hobbies underwent a drastic change—thanks to an innate sense of timing. I hastily made the transition from gridiron to dance floor when it became apparent that the boys were beginning to look on me as something more interesting than a scatback. Consequently, by the time I reached the eleventh grade, my enthusiasm for football had been channeled into cheerleading. For two years I gave vociferous vocal encouragement to the CHS Wildcats. The heat of excitement, however, sometimes causes us to revert to type. My father's favorite recollection of my cheerleading career concerned the night I was standing parallel with Clarksdale's star halfback when he caught a sideline pass at midfield and scampered toward a touchdown. Daddy claimed that I raced along the sidelines beside Swivelhips Salmon for forty yards—and was waiting impatiently in the end zone when he crossed the goal line!

After that rather involved preamble, I may still have to set the record straight: *I do not now, nor have I ever played professional football.* However, it happens that I am well acquainted with a number of people who do. So presently I shall climb into the Backseat and describe in story and song how and why the men of pro football choose and are chosen for this work—including some of the more telling incidents that happen to them along the way. (One picks up quite a few tidbits in thirteen years of snooping about the National Football League.)

First I must warn that a mild form of nepotism frequently rears its head during my reminiscences. I find it necessary to dwell extensively (though not exclusively) on the doings of a certain quarterback who is kin to me by marriage.

THE WEEK BEFORE: PRACTICE

Charlie has always claimed that he keeps coming back year after year only because I enjoy my autumn vacation in New York so much. The stay would indeed be a marvelous three-month holiday—if only the man of the house weren't obliged to indulge meanwhile in the liveliest of livelihoods.

The fans who think a professional football player earns his salary only on Sunday are now few in number. However, in days gone by, before the sport captured the imagination of the public, I was asked repeatedly: "What do the boys do with themselves between games?"

This is one misconception of which I am most tolerant, for I arrived on the scene back in 1949 with much the same question. I had visions of happy little jaunts with Charles to museums, art galleries, tall buildings, and other points of city interest. His curt reply to my astonished: "You mean you practice *every* day?" gave me the impression that I would be left to my own devices for sightseeing. And so I was.

I soon learned that the "game" is in reality a six-day-a-week job. Its participants are businessmen. Perhaps they differ from our concept of the gray flannel insurance salesman (a role many of them assume off-season, incidentally)—but there exist notable points of similarity to many other occupations. For instance, like the atomic scientist, the players must keep abreast of the latest enemy weapons. Like gangbusters, they love their work—else they could not risk loss of life and limb week after week. They keep bankers' hours. But, like the milkman, they must deliver the goods or be taken off the route!

Practice schedules during the season vary slightly from team to team, but most of them parallel that of the Giants. Since the boys don't close shop on Sunday, Monday is their day off. But even this respite must be interrupted occasionally by an early-morning trip to the Stadium, where Giant trainers stand ready to supply appropriate treatment for a variety of game-sustained injuries.

Tuesday is a light practice day. Movies of the previous Sunday's game are shown, with the offense and defense meeting separately for an hour and fifteen minutes or so. Unfortunately for those who didn't acquit themselves particularly well in the game, the projectors are equipped with backup gadgets which allow the coaches to call for certain plays to be run over and over until the reason for a play's failure—or its success—can be pinpointed.

The chief scout then presents his report on the team to be played the following week. I pity this valued member of the organization in one respect. Presumably a Giant fan, he sees his favorite team perform only once a year—in the last game of the season. For while the New Yorkers are at work in one stadium, he is stationed in another miles away studying future Giant opponents in action. Notebook in hand, he analyzes and records the strategy of the enemy, concentrating on recent innovations, unfamiliar personnel, and various refinements which might fail to show up in the game films.

A good scout has a "feel" for his work. His intuitive approach often enables him to ferret out details which no camera can capture completely. Frank Gifford, who retired briefly as a player after the 1960 season, scouted for the Giants in 1961. There is a distinct advantage in choosing a former player with *recent*, active service to serve in this capacity. Not only was Frank able to observe the games through the eyes of a skilled football analyst, he was qualified to sprinkle his report with inside observations based on experience. Having played against most of the members of the team he was scouting, he frequently offered helpful suggestions: "Old Danny has slowed up a half a step since last year. I think we can beat him deep."

The football scout employed by an opposing team was once treated with all the graciousness accorded an enemy spy in wartime. Nowadays, since all teams deem them essential, many clubs go so far as extending press box privileges to the men of the reconnaissance trade, expecting the same consideration in return, of course. The scout has put away his cloak, if not his dagger.

On Tuesday the players spend only thirty or forty minutes on the field. Since we live in the shadow of Yankee Stadium, Charlie arrives home in time for lunch.

Each day's outdoor practice begins with three laps around the field, a distance of well over a thousand yards.

Strenuous group calisthenics follow.

The scheduled "play practice" takes place.

And the session ends with a series of "wind sprints," in which players divide themselves informally into three "teams." (There are usually more than thirty-three participants.) As each center snaps the ball in turn, he and his group run down the field full tilt. There they regroup and repeat the procedure until the coach signals a return to the locker room.

Former Giant head coach Jim Lee Howell was a devout advocate of running as a beneficial preparation for combat. When he was promoted from end coach to the top position in 1954, one of the ends (long accustomed to Jim's concentration on this phase of training) announced to a group of backfield men: "It will be a real pleasure to see some of you other fellows do a little running for a change. Every end on the Giants could make the U.S. Olympic team in any long-distance event!"

Wednesdays and Thursdays are "brown bag" days. Since the players meet from ten in the morning to three-thirty in the afternoon, they usually come to practice with lunches packed in brown paper bags, cheerfully supplied by their wives.

In a strategy meeting the offensive team goes over the plays the coaches think will be most effective against the type of defense employed by the team coming up, with emphasis on circumventing strength and exploiting weaknesses of individual team members. The defense studies the opposing offense in another room. Players then don sweat clothes and work out on the field for about an hour and forty minutes. First the defense simulates the defense of the upcoming adversary, and the offense runs through its repertoire. Then they switch and the offense pretends to be that of the opponents while the defense goes through its paces. During these drills, defensive players put on yellow overblouses to distinguish them from members of the "opposing team."

He may not even be aware of it, but nearly every player has certain characteristics which distinguish his style of play. A tackle may customarily come across the line "high." Another may charge in "low." A secondary man may have a tendency to drop back unusually fast. These individual habits will be mimicked as closely as possible in practice sessions by the players representing particular opponents. An offensive "actor" does not assume merely the indefinite role of "the Colt quarterback." He becomes "Johnny Unitas," and tries to emulate both John's mannerisms and his deceptive tactics—such things as "pumping" the ball (feinting to throw) in the direction of several potential receivers before actually releasing it to his primary target. Incidentally, Charlie cannot duplicate this maneuver to perfection because his hands are too small. When he fakes a throw, he must pump the ball into his left hand, holding it with his right in order to reinforce his grip. John's long fingers enable him to hold the ball firmly in any position—a valuable aptitude comparable to the finesse of trick artists who can suspend a basketball from the palm of one hand.

There are several correct methods of fulfilling certain assignments. Each defensive tackle, for example, is assigned an area to cover. The manner in which he carries out this responsibility differs according to the individual. Frank Fuller of the St. Louis Cardinals is a "comer." With the snap of the ball he slashes straight ahead to get on with the business at hand. In contrast, Art Donovan of the Baltimore Colts is a "reader." He lurks in position for an instant, basing his move on the activity of the offensive guards, who usually lead the play. Both methods have merit. Both have weaknesses. The offensive team tries to capitalize on the weaknesses. All of which points up the importance of compiling (through films, scouting reports, and past experience) a "book" of advance information about "enemy" personnel.

The pepper chatter more commonly associated with baseball occurs during these trial-and-error practice sessions. The air is filled with singsong shouts of "Atta boy, Joe! Go get 'em, Ba—by!" (pass completed) or "Good play there, Cliffy Boy. All the way back, now. All the way back!" (pass intercepted). Playing for pay does not seem to dampen the boyish enthusiasm of these men of football.

Early in Charlie's career, when he was the only Giant quarterback, he had to do all of the practice passing—first directing the Giant attack, then that of the opponents. His arm stayed sore all week, and he considered Sunday almost a holiday because he had to pass just half as much as on other days. Now most teams customarily carry at least three quarterbacks. In fact, several years ago Charlie wrote from training camp: *There are so many men trying out for quarterback this year I'm not getting much practice. I have to stand around so long waiting for my turn, I've been running extra laps to keep in shape—and as you know, I'm not all that fond of running! Even my own roommate is trying to take my job away from me!*

This facetious reference to halfback Frank Gifford's fling at the quarterback position that summer brings to mind a conversation I had with Charles after Frank was unsuccessful in his bid. Tongue in cheek, I asked him one day: "Remember what delicious pound cakes that Mrs. Curtis from Clarksdale makes? Well, she'll gladly give the recipe to anyone who asks, but she's always careful to omit a vital ingredient so that the product turned out by her imitators lacks that 'certain something.' I often wonder if you did the same thing in tutoring Frank."

Taking me seriously, Charles said defensively, "Giff was doing *great*. He could have made it too. He just made the mistake of already being the best halfback in the league."

Following the offensive-defensive drills, the punting and place-kicking teams form and practice for twenty minutes or so. Afterwards the boys gather for lunch in the locker room which, by the way, has wall-to-wall carpeting. Among the stools and straight chairs occupied by the players during lunch and meetings, there are two lounge chairs. One is occupied on a first-come, first-served basis. The other is invariably left vacant until the "graying veteran" arrives—a show of respect by the players for their elders, I suppose. The Giants alternate with the New York Yankees in using the Stadium facilities. Charles points with pride to the coincidence that, during the baseball season, his locker belongs to Mickey Mantle—and, in days gone by, to Joe DiMaggio.

The fact that Giant players believe in the all-work-and-no-play adage is exemplified by the artwork which appears periodically (and anonymously) on the locker room bulletin board. Several years ago, for example, early-arriving squad members discovered three neatly typewritten sheets, a Shulmanesque satire entitled *The Saga of Carl Roth, Player of Football*. Excerpt:

My fearless, ferocious approach to the game stems from early training at home. There were twelve of us who sat down to the supper table each night. Dear old Mom encouraged us to be self-reliant by putting only eleven pork chops on the platter. . . .

Kyle Rote swore then and swears now that he was not the author of this whimsical gem. But, he is still occasionally called "Carl" by teammates.

A year or two ago, a full-page picture of Dick Nolan appeared in newspaper advertisements for a brand of cigarettes. Soon after, his likeness was emblazoned on a fifty-foot billboard in the heart of Times Square. Displayed prominently in the locker room the next day—alongside a copy of the newspaper ad—was a letter, purportedly written to Dick by the president of the cigarette company. It read in part: *The other board members and I don't mind your standing in front of the sign for several hours each day smoking our cigarettes. But setting up a card table there on Forty-second Street and signing autographs is going a bit far . . .*

Defensive halfback Dick Lynch (then a bachelor) evoked envy by appearing in public one night with glamorous actress Kim Novak on his arm. Next day the bulletin board was a thing of beauty. Dorothy Kilgallen's newspaper column headlining the momentous event was surrounded by Novak pin-up pictures. Below, crayoned in large block letters, was the cryptic observation of an anonymous teammate: "In one date with Dick, Kim learned more defensive maneuvers than Lynch has been able to absorb in two whole years as a pro."

After lunch, movies of the next opponent in action are shown. Once it was illegal for a club to view the movies of a game in which it had not taken part; but the rule was impractical to enforce, and films are now swapped freely about the league. As soon as the movies of Sunday's game have been viewed by the participating teams (usually on Tuesday), a round-robin exchange begins. Each team ships last Sunday's movies to next Sunday's opponent.

Films play a doubly important role in briefing players about an *unfamiliar* opponent. Since an Eastern Conference team will seldom meet the same Western Conference team oftener than once every three or four years, squads from opposite conferences naturally know far less about each other than about the teams they encounter twice a season.

Movies of each game are carefully divided into offensive and defensive sections. To save time during practice sessions, a player is shown only that portion of the film which documents the type of action which will confront him in the upcoming game against a certain opponent. Therefore, for example, the Giant defensive men see the Cleveland offense at work, while the offensive men watch only the Cleveland defensive maneuvers. Even the punts and kick-offs are deleted and shown only to players who are members of the kicking and receiving squads! Another manifestation of the high degree of specialization which is characteristic of the pro game. And there's more. Formerly the films were laboriously cut and spliced by hand in order to separate the various phases of activity. In stride with the times, the Giant management eliminated this bothersome patchwork by employing a system of two-platoon cameras—one shooting only offense; the other, only defense.

During training camp players scrimmage daily; but when the regular season begins, body contact is suspended. With the league allowing each team to carry only thirty-six men, injuries during a game are sufficiently frequent without tempting fate in practice.

Often a team that is behind in score will discover that its most formidable opponent is not the adamant group of men on the opposite side of the scrimmage line, but an inanimate enemy: the clock. In order to refine the procedure of executing the maximum number of plays in a limited amount of time, the Giants participate once a week in a series of "two-minute drills." Racing against a stopwatch, the quarterback selects his calls from a group of plays concocted especially for use during the last two minutes of each half. Game conditions are simulated as nearly as possible in order to accustom the players to the urgency of the situation and to eliminate waste motion on game day.

Players must learn to take the two-minute plays in "shorthand." Ordinarily, the quarterback calls out the pass patterns in the huddle, delineating the assignments of each eligible receiver. "Green. Flanker right. L(eft) and R(ight) cross. Wing trail. B shoot. On 2," he might say. When time is fleeting, he indicates the same play with a mere: "80 left. On 2."

Friday, activity tapers off. Players spend an hour on the field, concentrating principally on blocking assignments and on "automatics" to be called by the quarterback to combat shifting defenses.

Saturday's session constitutes a quick warm-up and a rehash of punt and kick-off returns. In recent years, Saturday has evolved into "family day" at the Stadium. As the weekend approaches, the team children (male variety) take a sanctimonious interest in washing behind *both* ears, putting their toys away, and avoiding (whenever possible) teasing their little sisters. For in most families the reward for good behavior during the week is going to practice with Daddy on Saturday.

While the players are engaged in the business of the day, Giant trainer Sid Moret volunteers to oversee the activities of the little people. He explains to his wide-eyed charges the workings of the mysterious therapeutic gadgets over which he presides, teaches the youngsters to tape their ankles, and referees the peewee game which takes place on the sidelines while the big people are at work on the field—all the while subtly offering pointers in good sportsmanship. Ask any little Giant to name the two greatest sports figures in the whole wide world, and he will likely reply, "Daddy and Sid."

And then there is Sunday.

{8}

THE HOUR BEFORE: LOCKER ROOM

Do professional football players get stage fright? Or are these brawny craftsmen, having reached the height of their profession, immune to temperamental attacks of butterflies? An informal survey of Giant players unearthed an almost unanimous admission to some degree of nervousness on the day of the game. None seem the least hesitant to acknowledge it—a fact that would tend to rule out the presumption that this emotion is one associated with amateurism.

The manifestations of pre-game tension vary from player to player. Oddly, those who are normally rather reserved are apt to become exuberant men-in-motion and chatter excitedly with anyone who will listen. On the other hand, those usually extroverted tend to withdraw— to become solemn and silent as game time approaches.

Let's examine a typical game day. Most players sleep later than on a practice day. A mid-morning brunch takes the place of the regular noontime meal, since eating too near game time might have dire consequences. Many players prefer a hearty meal of steak and potatoes, since it must suffice until nightfall. However, Charles, a scanty eater at all times, requests an ordinary breakfast, usually bacon and eggs. He eschews pancakes as too heavy and orange juice as mildly upsetting.

Most sleep well the night before, but begin to vibrate almost immediately after awakening. Punter Don Chandler's first move is to the window of his apartment, which overlooks Yankee Stadium. He checks the flags displayed there. Thus he gets an immediate indication of how the wind velocity will affect his punting.

Says fullback Alex Webster, "Sure I'm nervous. My stomach stays in knots from the moment I open my eyes in the morning until I first make contact. Then I'm okay. You may remember that last week Charlie's first pass was incomplete. It was supposed to be thrown to me, but I was so tense that I fouled up my pattern and he had to throw it away. That's probably why some teams choose to kick off, hoping the receivers will be nervous on the first play and fumble." Alex never shaves before a game. Most players will concede only that they ordinarily follow the same ritual each Sunday, but a few admit to definite superstitions. Pat Summerall insists on wearing the same outfit to the Stadium for every game—sport coat, slacks, shoes, even underwear. A crisis arose several years ago. The cleaners failed to return his coat. He dashed to the shop late Saturday afternoon and caught the owner just as he was locking up for the night. Pat kicked three field goals that afternoon—one a forty-nine-yarder.

Defensive end Jim Katcavage has a "thing" about being first. He rushes into the training room with his hands outstretched to have his wrists taped first. On road trips he always boards the first bus; and upon arriving at the field, the players stand aside in the aisle for fear Kat will trample them in his anxiety to be the first one to disembark.

Most of the players arrive at the Stadium about eleven thirty or twelve o'clock on game day. Summerall is usually the third one there at eleven o'clock. Dick Nolan is second at ten. Katcavage finally gave up on this "first." Cliff Livingston, the earliest bird of all, opens shop at eight-thirty. "It takes me quite a while to get myself in the proper frame of mind," says Cliff. The former U.C.L.A. ace accomplishes this by lounging on a couch in an anteroom with his feet propped up, his play book resting on his lap, his eyes partially closed, staring at the ceiling. A radio is tuned to a station which constantly plays soothing music. His teammates don't bother speaking to Cliff; they know he probably won't answer.

As the players arrive by twos and threes, they take brief note of the bulletin board which exhibits an article from a national magazine headlined: "Why the Browns Will Win the Championship." The boys amble over to their lockers, strip, and sit around discussing the previous day's college games while waiting to be taped. (Failure to have both ankles taped for a game or scrimmage could result in a $250 fine; needless to say, the owners don't want to have their valuable property damaged.)

On the surface, the atmosphere is quite jovial until the one o'clock buzzer rings, a signal for members of the press and anyone else not directly connected with the team to leave. The boys call it, half seriously, the panic button. A hush falls over the locker room. Signs of tension become more evident. Players don their togs in silence and a few minutes later trot onto the field for the pre-game exercises.

This warm-up period serves a double purpose in the case of Pat Summerall. Besides loosening up his kicking leg, Pat is testing his power in relation to the wind velocity. Afterwards he holds a short conference with the coach and estimates for him the maximum distance he can attain from both ends of the field. For instance, Pat might say, "I can kick it sixty yards, maybe more, toward the outfield. But the wind is so bad the other way, I don't think I could reach over forty." It is this information that colors the coach's decisions during the game concerning the choice between a field goal attempt and a punt.

The use of baseball terminology in distinguishing between the ends of the football field (infield-outfield) and between the sides (first base-third base) is not as incongruous as it seems. Most professional games are played in temporarily converted baseball parks; and being a rectangle, the football field has no such distinctive markings of its own.

Gridiron tacticians discovered some years ago that confusion was lessened immeasurably all around when both teams knew a few minutes in advance which team would receive the opening kick-off. Therefore, toward the end of the loosening-up period, just before the teams return to the locker room for their last minute conclaves, co-captains

Kyle Rote and Andy Robustelli meet unobtrusively on the sidelines with the referee and opposing captains for the toss of the coin. Until two years ago the captains acted out a window-dressing flip in the center of the field immediately prior to the kick-off. Unsuspecting fans assumed this to be genuine. In accordance with the new rule, the captains merely shake hands (omitting the second toss), and the referee indicates the result through pantomime.

It may be significant that the change in procedure occurred shortly after television networks sought to cleanse their electronic souls by "protecting" the public from all wicked behind-the-scenes chicanery—like canned laughter, for instance. I think the omission of this harmless duplication (the pseudotoss) robs the game of a certain amount of pre-game suspense. In order to avoid offending the literal-minded spectator, field announcers could precede the meaningless re-enactment with: "This flip was pre-recorded."

Upon returning to the locker room the players glance at the blackboard. The result of the toss is written there: "Receiving in the infield." The offense and defense then split up and hold eleventh-hour briefings. It is now, for instance, that head coach Al Sherman announces whether the opening call will be a razzle-dazzle "home run" play designed to go all the way—or something less sensational.

Afterwards, with fifteen minutes remaining before game time, the players settle down in front of their lockers for the final wait. An air of tense anticipation now

pervades the room. Most sit quietly, but invariably Dick
Nolan rushes up to poker-faced Jimmy Patton, the field
leader of the defensive backs, for a frantic conference. In
the background Jim Katcavage savagely attacks a post
first with one padded shoulder, then the other.

Coach Sherman announces ominously: "Ten more
minutes." Rosie Grier, who up to now has been the
calmest of all, turns a little green around the gills and
hastily retreats to the bathroom. Charlie begins his last-
minute coughing spasm. Phil King sits absently tearing
adhesive tape into strips, wadding them up and hurling
them to the floor with a vengeance. Dick Modzelewski is
occupied with replacing his small contact lenses with the
old-fashioned larger ones, which are less likely to scratch
his eyeball should he be smacked in the eye.

"Five more minutes." Tension mounts. Kyle Rote and
Joe Walton hurriedly seek out the starting quarterback to
check once more on what automatics he is likely to call.

Tom Scott, grimacing fiercely, practices his game face.

Cliff continues to stare into space.

"Gather round now." The spell is broken as Sherman
quietly delivers a brief pep talk. The histrionics of a college coach would be ridiculed here. Al confines his parting
shot to cold fact: "If we expect to win the championship,
we must play like champions."

At its conclusion, someone shouts: "Let's go get 'em!"
And the team charges toward the field with a whoop and
a holler.

{9}

THE GAME

"And from Baylor University—Del Shofner!" the field announcer exclaims. The crowd sets up a cheer and begins to buzz with anticipation as the starting teams break formation on the field and retreat to the sidelines for last-minute instructions and impromptu gymnastics. Some players bounce around doing knee bends and diminutive wind sprints. Others take turns banging each other on the shoulders to lessen the shock of initial contact with the enemy and establish the mood.

If Summerall is kicking off, he stabs repeatedly at an imaginary ball. If the Giants are receiving, the starting quarterback tosses a few short passes to an end or halfback standing in place on the sidelines. Usually a player at the passer's side receives the throw back and hands him the ball to prevent his hands from becoming overly chafed or numbed by repeated catches.

Line coach Ed Kohlman stands by with a clipboard on which the various teams are listed: regular offensive, regular defensive, kick-off, punting, and the kick-off and punting receiving teams. Players are briefed beforehand in the locker room concerning their duties for the day; but since lineups vary slightly from week to week, a man who is assigned to several of the specialized teams might wish to consult the clipboard for verification.

At 2:05 the opposing teams take the field, turning to face the flag as "The Star-Spangled Banner" reverberates throughout the Stadium. During the anthem I offer a silent prayer that no one on either team will be hurt. I never pray for victory, leaving the outcome of the games to skill and chance.

" . . . and the home of the brave." The brave is almost drowned out by the shrieks and whistles of expectant fans. The referee blows his whistle, the kicker booms the ball downfield, and the game is underway.

The least attractive chore is participation in the kick-offs and punts. In fact, players on the kicking teams call themselves "the kamikazi squad." Running full speed in spread formation as the assignment requires leaves the members of the "suicide squad" vulnerable to surprise attack, and the most serious injuries occur when the player is hit unexpectedly, or "from his blind side," as football jargon has it.

Following the reception and return of the kick, "the fruit basket upsets" as kick-off and receiving squads are replaced by the regular offensive and defensive units. Mass substitution, the trademark of the professional game, has tended to lessen the importance of the triple-threat player as such; but the resulting specialization affords an excellence of execution not possible under limited substitution rules.

On most pro teams (the Giants included) the quarterback shoulders the responsibility of directing the attack. Naturally, he doesn't make up the plays as he goes along. Far from it. The plays at his command are the product of hours of meticulous planning by the coaches and hours of "rehearsal" on the practice field. In his general repertoire there are hundreds of variations, but in any given game his choice is usually limited to twenty or thirty calls—plays carefully selected as the ones most likely to succeed against a particular opponent and therefore polished during the preceding week of practice. It is from this narrowed selection that he usually chooses, for it would be extremely risky to dust off a play unused for months and suddenly present it in the huddle. One of the ten might have forgotten exactly how it went—or the quarterback himself might waste an instant in fatal uncertainty.

Though the offensive coach generally dictates the type of strategy he expects the quarterback to employ, he rarely calls more than a small percentage of the specific plays. However, when he does suggest a play (by sending in a substitute with the message or talking with the quarterback during a time out), he is reasonably confident that the quarterback will carry out his orders.

There have been exceptions. Once when Steve Owen was head coach of the Giants, a cocky young quarterback defied his orders to run the ball on first down. Instead the rookie threw a pass, which was intercepted. Steve restrained his ire until the game was over.

"Son," Owen drawled, "didn't you hear me say to hand the ball off to Eddie on that first play?"

"Yessir, but I thought . . ."

"I ought to fine you a hundred dollars!"

"Why don't you make it *two* hundred?" blurted the hot-tempered rookie.

"All right. Two hundred."

"Well just make it two *thousand!*"

"Suits me," Steve replied placidly.

"Why not make it *ten* thousand, then!" A faint blush which had begun at the back of his neck now colored the youngster's whole face.

Steve smiled for the first time. "Son, you don't make that much."

Steve came from the old school of rock-'em-sock-'em football and never quite accepted the new text of wide-open, high-scoring tactics. He said often, "I'd rather beat a team 3–0 than 37–3." I don't believe he ever quite convinced himself that the forward pass was fair. Such conservatism, coupled with a marked concentration on defense, undoubtedly curtailed Charlie's potential effectiveness during this period. However, even now he bristles when some well-meaning soul points up this notion, for Charlie still retains a deep affection and respect for "Stout Steve" Owen.

The coach patrols the sidelines in front of the bench, trying to keep up with what is going on. Occasionally a visitor from the hometown expresses a yen to "sit on the bench with the players." Charlie's reply is discouraging: "There are a total of four sideline passes available to the players each week. But if Robustelli—he's co-captain—hasn't promised all of them, I'll get you one. However, I wouldn't recommend it. If it's the players you want to see, I'll take you to practice one day. If it's the game you want to see, let me get you a ticket in the stands. The bench is the worst seat in the house."

"Do you really think the bench is the worst seat in the house?" I asked him one day.

"Certainly. You can't see half of what is going on. That's one reason I think it is unwise for a coach to call every play. Even with help from upstairs, [the telephone observer high in the stands] I don't think the coach on the sidelines can grasp the continuing situation as well as the quarterback on the field. Not only does the quarterback have the advantage of being on the scene, he can profit from the on-the-spot observations of his teammates."

"'My halfback is drifting inside,' Kyle Rote might say. 'I think I can beat him on a down-and-out.' And when the right time comes, I call a down-and-out pass to Kyle. Experienced linemen like Wietecha and Stroud also give you good suggestions."

"Of course you have to take the advice of some players with a grain of salt. Remember Eddie Price? Steady Eddie was a dandy little fullback. Mighty powerful for his size. But according to Eddie, he could beat his man on every single play. We never went into the huddle that he didn't beg for the ball. I think he would have been glad to carry it every time we lined up if I had just let him."

Despite the mental strain which, Charlie notes, far exceeds the physical demands of the game, the quarterback who is allowed freedom of play selection gives his team a definite advantage. "But you can't argue with the amazing success of a coach like [Cleveland's] Paul Brown, who sends in every play from the bench," he adds.

"Naturally I can't take in all the phases of action when I am on the field. That's where our telephone system comes into play." Here Charlie was referring to the system of communication through which one of the assistant coaches (usually end coach Ken Kavanaugh) sits in the press box and talks with one of the quarterbacks stationed at a table near the bench. From up there Ken sometimes is able to detect flaws that might not be apparent at field level. The "phone man" on the bench (usually a quarterback who is not playing that day) relays Ken's information to the coaches and/or players. Often the playing quarterback will sit down for a person-to-person chat while his defensive teammates are on the field.

The Giants also use on-the-spot photography in recording significant or unexpected changes in formation. Giant vice-president Wellington Mara frequently doubles as cameraman. From the highest tier he trains a Polaroid camera on the action below and drops the finished pictures down to the bench in a weighted sock. For years, on seeing these foreign objects sail periodically past our section, I thought disgruntled fans in the gallery above us were attempting to bombard Giant players with unfriendly missiles.

The action on the field is what spectators pay to see, but they are missing an intriguing part of the game if they fail to note occasionally the bustle of activity on the bench.

Offensive players usually occupy one section of the bench; defensive players, the other. This informal seating arrangement has several advantages. In the heat of battle, coaches can locate certain players quickly. Also, players can find each other without wasting precious seconds. A man leaving the game may wish to hold a hurried conference with his replacement in order to give him the benefit of recent experience—or perhaps a second-stringer on the bench has a word of advice for his counterpart, having noticed something of value only another center (for instance) would detect. Sitting together gives the specialists belonging to a certain unit the opportunity of discussing previous mistakes and analyzing the prevailing weakness of the opponents.

The half-dozen men in street clothes sitting on either end of the bench are holders of sideline passes, friends of the owners or players. The other non-players hovering nearby render various services during the game. Dr. Francis Sweeny leads the corps of official attendants. He sits tense and watchful—his little black bag filled with whatever little black bags are filled with; his head filled with caustic comments with which to berate the game officials foolish enough to wander too close to his lair.

The Giants also employ a squad of trainers and equipment men who minister to the lesser needs of the players. The tools of their trades are many. The water bucket, with its communal dipper, stands ready. At the "time out" signal, the water boy grabs it and streaks for the field. Actually, drinking the water is taboo. "Bad for your system!" Doc wheezes. Players are supposed to squish it around in the mouth, then spit it out. However, few can resist the temptation to sneak a swallow or two. During time outs the trainers clean the cleats of those who request this service and distribute wet towels with which the players wipe their faces.

Their pseudo-medical kits contain ice bags, applied immediately to bruises and sprains to prevent hemorrhaging and keep down swelling; ammonia capsules; a variety of bandages; and rolls and rolls of adhesive tape.

Various accessories aid players in combating the rigors of cold weather. The bench is equipped with an electric blanket or two and with handwarmers which generate heat with lighter fluid. Players wear wool underwear, but donning "long handles" does not solve the principal problem: icy hands and feet. The most effective method of allaying this botheration was provided by a citizen from the mid-South. Several years ago he made the Giants a present of half a dozen old-fashioned charcoal buckets which were placed at intervals along the bench. While not in action, players can at least thaw out temporarily.

Linemen ordinarily wear gloves to prevent frostbite; but ends and backfield men, who handle the ball, cannot afford to restrict the use of hands and fingers by bundling them up. Because the quarterback handles the ball on every play, digital numbness is for him a serious handicap.

Five or six years ago Al Sherman suggested an innovation employed with success in the Canadian League, where he had recently been a coach—a pair of skintight golf gloves. However, golf gloves do not come in pairs. The right-handed golfer wears a glove only on his *left* hand, and a *right*-hand glove is difficult to come by—even during the height of the golfing season. Finding one of each in mid-December might be likened to the twelve tasks of Hercules. Persistence was crowned with success. The gloves arrived in time for use in a chilly encounter. Charlie put them on and went into action. "They really did help," he recalls, "and I was thinking: 'Why didn't we think of this before?' Just then I fumbled. We recovered the ball; but when I went back to the huddle, one of the larger linemen grumbled, 'Get those things off!' I really don't think the gloves had anything to do with my fumbling, but I didn't want those guys mad at me. I took them off."

The equipment men also stand guard over the twelve balls which the home team is required to furnish for each game. In wet weather the offensive team captain may call for replacing a waterlogged ball with a dry one. At that, a dozen balls would seem to meet the demand handsomely. However, some parks are so constructed that a ball sailing over the goal post invariably lands in the stands. The scramble of spectators to retrieve the "souvenir" often is profitless, for the park policemen have orders to repossess straying balls if at all possible (and generally are booed heartily for their efforts).

Although a regulation ball costs $17.35, this policy is not dictated entirely by economy. Consider how rapidly the supply would diminish in a high-scoring game played in a park with a "short fence." I suspect that the Redskin management became extremely nervous when such a situation arose in the 1949 Giant-Washington game played in Griffith Stadium. The end zone stand at one end of the field was occupied almost entirely by sailors—hundreds of them. Whenever a ball landed among the maze of uniforms it was as good as lost, for the ball sleuths were not able to identify the filcher in the usual manner: by his clothing. The Redskin equipment men fidgeted as the supply of balls dwindled. Fortunately the game ended just in time. Giants 45, Redskins 35. Lost footballs: 11.

As players return from the field of action, the equipment men make sure each one has a cape to throw around his shoulders to prevent cooling off too quickly. They also preside over the spare parts. This emergency equipment includes extra chin straps, elbow pads, jerseys, shoe laces, and other items most likely to fall into disrepair.

Eye black, a sort of soot in paste form, is sometimes applied beneath the eyes to diminish the sun's glare. The descriptive phrase "glue-fingered receivers" is not entirely metaphorical. Tacky paste is available to pass receivers, who may wish to place a blob of the stickum on an inside ankle, and coat their hands periodically to improve traction.

The equipment man's bag of tricks also includes such improbable items as tea towels. In wet weather the man playing center acts as a towel rack. Hanging from the back of his "belt" and over his rump is a small towel on which the quarterback dries his hands each time before handling the ball.

I'm sure you have noticed that after the final gun sounds, very often several opposing players suddenly lay animosity aside and walk off the field together chatting amiably. Usually they are either alumni of the same college or former employees of the same pro team. Sometimes they are brothers (for example, Ray and Barney Poole, Dick and Ed Modzelewski, Lew and Preston Carpenter).

In a Giant-Cardinal game several years ago there was an amusing variation on this theme. It was time out. Kyle Rote lay in a heap. He had been clobbered after making a sensational catch on the four-yard line. While the players of both teams milled about nervously, Charlie was peering anxiously over the shoulders of Dr. Sweeny and the trainers as they ministered to the unconscious form of our team captain. Just then someone tapped Charles on the back. It was Billy Stacey, a Cardinal rookie recently of Mississippi State (Old Miss's traditional rival). Billy stuck out his hand and said, "It's a great pleasure to meet you, Mr. Conerly. I've been an admirer of yours ever since I can remember." Unaccustomed to such friendliness from an opponent *during* a game, ("What would the fans think?") Charlie was taken aback for a second, but recovered his aplomb in time to return the greeting. He wouldn't admit it, but I'm certain that being called "Mr. Conerly" unnerved Charles far more than the ill-timed salutation itself. Kyle got up, but it took Charlie a little longer to recover.

THE GAME FROM THE STANDS

Who admires the brilliant faking of an end for whom the pass is *not* intended?

Who notices that the agile footwork of a certain defensive halfback was responsible for the fact that the opposing quarterback was forced to "eat the ball" in lieu of passing it as intended?

Who shouts, "Holding!" a full five seconds before the umpire throws down the penalty flag?

Who beholds with pride the crushing block that springs a halfback loose for a substantial gain?

Who observes the sometimes unhappy fate of the quarterback *after* he throws the ball?

For answers to the preceding questions, turn to Section 24, rows D and E in the mezzanine stands of Yankee Stadium. There sits a perceptive group that (collectively) misses little of what transpires on the field and on the bench—the wives and children of Giant players.

The managements of some teams purposely scatter the players' wives about the stands—the theory being that the keen competition existing between some players could lead to tense situations involving their spouses. The Giant organization does not hold with such pessimism. Giant wives sit together—with entirely satisfactory results so far. We find that unpleasantness in this—as in most situations—can be avoided by prudence and tact. The Golden Rule helps, too.

The wives themselves heartily endorse the "togetherness." Such a seating arrangement makes it possible for them to commiserate or jubilate—as the fortunes of the day might warrant.

Most arrive early enough to visit with the wives seldom seen during the week. We move up and down the rows exchanging theater reviews, admiring new outfits, inquiring about the health of children, and/or husbands injured in the previous week's game, and swapping tales of recent success in our second favorite sport—celebrity-spotting.

I like to be in my seat in time to see the pre-game warmup. Somehow it has the effect of breaking me in gently for the events to follow. I don't *feel* any older (even in the presence of fresh young wives still wearing their sorority pins), but the last thirteen years have had a dreadful effect on my nervous system. After giving Charlie a good-luck kiss as he departs for the Stadium about eleven thirty, I try to erase from my mind for as long as possible the unsettling fact that we really are playing a game that day. Whenever my thoughts disobey this ostrichism, a butterfly with clammy wings does a quadruple somersault and I am very likely to arrive at my seat in the Stadium slightly feverish and wearing mismated shoes.

One might think I'd get used to the tension after seeing almost a hundred Giant games. (I haven't missed a home game since arriving on the scene in 1949). But that butterfly gets friskier with each passing year. In the early days it never occurred to me that the Giants might lose or that Charlie might turn in anything less than a perfect performance or that he might be injured. I am still outrageously optimistic, but I now know that such things *can* happen.

The Giants management reserves for the players' wives the choicest seats in the Stadium; the section stretches between the forty- and fifty-yard lines in the mezzanine, which is covered to thwart the elements. Each of us occupies the same seat all season and, generally, from one year to the next.

For each home game a player receives one free ticket for his wife and one for each child old enough to attend— no more. The cost of other tickets procured by a player for friends or acquaintances is deducted from his paycheck. He must also pay for his wife's ticket when she travels to an out-of-town game. This is as it should be.

However, the prevailing misapprehension that each player receives a fistful of free tickets for each game has caused Charlie and his colleagues considerable expense over the years. Friends understand the situation, but Charlie has finally learned from sad and costly experience to avoid obtaining tickets indiscriminately for doubtful acquaintances ("You wouldn't remember me, but I was a freshman when you were a senior at Ole Miss . . ."). The risk has also been lessened by the fact that advance sales to Giant games have been brisk in recent years. A player therefore has little chance of obtaining more than six tickets to each game, the number set aside for each player to buy if he wishes.

I have preached the one-free-ticket-and-that-one-is-mine gospel so often that my thoroughness sometimes returns to embarrass us. Many times people whom we have invited to be our guests at a game have been so brainwashed by my sermon that they become violent when Charlie refuses to accept reimbursement for their tickets!

Some wives admittedly do not understand the game as well as others do. "It's no wonder that I know so little about football," Betty Rote once confided. "I never go to a football game with a man—only with another girl who doesn't understand the game any better than I do—present company excepted," she added. "And it has been that way forever. With the exception of a few minor tiffs during adolescence, Kyle and I have gone steady since we were five years old. From junior high football right on up, while the other girls were asking their dates on-the-spot questions, I was sitting in the stands cheering my date-by-proxy (but not proximity) on to another touchdown."

"For years I have been intending to ask Kyle to sit down and fill me in on the finer points of the game. But I'm afraid it's too late for that now. I have an idea that his reply to my first question would be something like: 'Good heavens, Betty! If you don't know any more about the game than that, why have you bothered going all these years?' "

"So when the discussion of the day's game becomes too specific, I guess I'll have to continue to bluff my way through by smiling sweetly and being an excellent listener."

Actually Betty was exaggerating. She understands the game very well—certainly better than the average woman. However, the whimsical analysis of her own situation points up an occupational hazard not uncommon among football wives (present company *included*): that of knowing less about the technical aspects of the game than the general public might assume—and being hesitant to reveal this lack by asking "stupid questions."

I would guess that the wife of a defensive player probably has a better grasp of the game as a whole, for she is not as prone to "watch the ball" as are her "offensive" sisters. Lack of knowledge has nothing to do with lack of enthusiasm in our case. All of us know enough about the game to cheer lustily in the right places. Points of confusion are passed along the row for clarification, and such questions seldom travel far before receiving an answer or at least an opinion, which is relayed back down the row.

We have also learned to shuttle hot dogs along to starving children and complete transactions with the vendor without taking our eyes from the field. Many of the wives join the picnic, but food to me at this point has little appeal. A cup of coffee in extremely cold weather is about all I can manage.

During halftime we exchange greetings with the anonymous season ticket holders nearby whom we recognize as having occupied the same seats for years. Often friends sitting in other sections come to call. The wives sometimes talk over the action in the first half, and sometimes rush to finish a juicy story interrupted by the end of a recent time out. They need the halftime respite almost as much as the players and it ends all too soon.

An injury rings down a curtain of watchful silence on our group. All eyes trail the injured player from the field to the bench, then turn a sympathetic gaze toward his wife. The wife at her side strives to think of an encouraging comment. "I think he just got the wind knocked out of him. See—Doc is poking an ammonia capsule under his nose. I don't think it is his knee again. He didn't seem to be limping." Those close by nod approvingly.

The spell is broken as the wife of a little-used substitute gasps, "Omigosh—*John's* going in the game!"

A stranger sitting behind the wife of the injured player hands her a pair of binoculars, and she keeps them trained on her husband as action gets underway again. The rest of us return to the game but glance periodically at the bench. If the player is assisted to the locker room or fails to return to the game in a reasonable length of time, either Jack Mara, Giant president, or Father Dudley, the unofficial team chaplain, thoughtfully seeks out the anxious wife and gives her a first-hand report.

The gayer moments in the game are accompanied by a chorus of squeals and shouts; and the wife whose husband makes a touchdown, recovers a fumble, blocks a kick, or intercepts a pass accepts the plaudits of her excited neighbors with becoming immodesty. I wish the team fathers could see the pride such an accomplishment engenders in their youngsters.

At a game several years ago one of our defensive ends threw the opposing quarterback for a huge loss, thereby putting a game-winning field goal out of enemy reach. Forgotten for a moment in the flurry of noisy congratulations being directed at the lineman's wife, was the tousled-haired youngster, seven or eight years old, sitting at her side. Turning to a stranger sitting behind him he said softly, "That's my dad did that. *I'm* Andy Robustelli's boy."

{11}

AFTER THE GAME

After the game some wives wait for their husbands outside the dressing room, but most hurry up the hill to the hotel to begin dressing for our night "out." (No practice on Monday.) Though I would love to rush forward and claim Charles in view of the impressionable fans gathered there—especially after a win!—I must bolt for home as the final gun sounds, for our apartment is traditionally GHQ for the post-game interlude. Several of the wives who live in the suburbs change there from game clothes to dinner wear and remain to rendezvous with their player-husbands. This informal get-together is not an invitational affair. Those who can come and wish to, do. Giant couples who reside in the building wander in and out to check on who is going where for dinner. Once assembled, players gather in knots to rehash the game and wives who live "out" exchange chitchat.

I fear I am not of much assistance in supplying the suburbanites with news, for whenever possible I station myself within earshot of a game conversation. It is here that I garner a host of interesting sidelights that tight-lipped Charles will undoubtedly neglect to mention. Such tidbits as the reason the Giants nearly fumbled away the first home game in 1959. It seems, Alex Webster relates, that the brand-new jerseys were made of a material that is very slick before it is laundered. The shiny surface afforded no traction for the ball as it was held against the ball carriers' bodies, and on five occasions it had squirted loose.

Another night I find the answer to a question that had sent a murmur through the stands a few seconds before halftime that day. I eavesdrop while Pat Summerall explains why the Giants refused a five-yard penalty which would have moved them that much closer to the opponents' goal. "With time running out, Jim Lee [the coach] sent me in to try a field goal from the ten-yard line. I had a rather bad angle to shoot from as it was, and bringing the ball five yards closer to the goal post would merely have increased the disadvantage."

Dick Modzelewski volunteers an ironic bit of information gleaned from the Stadium groundskeepers—that good weather was responsible for the poor footing on the field that day! Ordinarily by this time of year cool days and nights have caused the Stadium grass to become coarse and tough, thereby providing traction for the runners. However, with temperatures consistently hovering in the 70s and 80s, the grass, blissfully unaware that the middle of October had arrived, retained its fine, spring-like texture. Throughout the evening, I pass this information along in conversation with various civilian-type acquaintances who invariably marvel at how observant I am. I customarily shrug modestly.

Following a loss, the prevailing mood is understandably somewhat less than ecstatic. But seldom can it be classed as one of gloom. Players seem to take a what's-done-is-done attitude toward the afternoon's misfortunes, and the conversation generally takes a rapid turn toward next week. Someone usually manages to brighten the atmosphere by recalling at least one humorous incident pertaining to the day's game. For instance, there was absolutely nothing amusing about being tied by the winless Dallas Cowboys in 1960. However, Cowboy owner Clint Murchison's post-game remark brought a smile to the lips of every frustrated Giant who heard it quoted later. As the final gun sounded, the ecstatic Mr. M. sighed in mock disappointment: "Well, you can't win 'em all."

Or perhaps it is necessary to think back for a bit of sunshine. An out-of-town visitor brings up the subject of air travel and excess baggage, thereby reminding the players to chide halfback Phil King. Phil, a weightlifting addict, decided one year to bring his barbells and allied equipment to training camp. Coals to Newcastle, but he was determined. Once aboard the plane, Phil did a quick bit of ciphering. The overweight charges he was obliged to pay totaled almost twice the cost of a new set of weights! Had he been a poor sport and remained silent about the incident, he would have robbed his colleagues of many hours of glee at his expense.

Since the Concourse Plaza is so close to Yankee Stadium, friends and friends of friends drop by to say hello and kill time while the game crowd abates and taxis become available. Consequently, there is sometimes an interesting array of outsiders in the Conerly apartment on a Sunday night. The arrival of our dear friends Baby and Toots Shor (the restaurateur) usually means excellent fortune, for Toots seems to know everybody in the world—and tries to make them all into Giant fans. He often has a sports personality in tow (Stan Musial, Eddie Arcaro, Cary Middlecoff) and sometimes gives us pleasure by bringing along a show business "name." Ordinarily we have but one star at a time to ogle, but occasionally the wives are confounded by two or three. On such occasions I make every effort to corral the hapless celebrities in the same corner of the room, so we can gawk at all of them at once.

One of the most successful nights (as voted by the wives) featured Gordon MacRae, who came with Toots, and David Niven, who arrived with our friend, drama critic John McClain. Amazingly, the two celebrities seemed as impressed by meeting the players present as vice versa. A few minutes after arriving, Gordon sought me out to ask, "When is Kyle Rote getting here? I've been a fan of his for such a long time, I must meet him." David (I didn't call him that—I couldn't decide whether to call him "David" or "Mr. Niven," so I didn't call him anything) cornered the players one by one to ask intelligent questions about the differences between rugby and football. He is a new fan of pro football and seemingly an ardent one. I'm afraid the boys did a much better job of being blasé than the wives, but Mr. Niven, David, that is, has a pair of the most startlingly blue eyes . . .

I have a feeling my mother still doesn't believe me when I write that we entertained such favorites of hers as Don Ameche or John Daly in our home. And sometimes I find it rather difficult to believe myself!

By the time the dinner hour approaches, players have "unwound" sufficiently to become interested in food. The where-shall-we-eat? chatter begins in earnest, and couples leave by twos and threes. The division of the troops is dictated sometimes by palship, sometimes by restaurant preference. The parting "see-you-laters" are not idle, for many players and wives will gather at one of our favorite after-dinner haunts. There once again the conversation turns to the game of the day, and I manage to find new ears. The waiters, aware of my propensity for celebrity-spotting, kindly alert me whenever one arrives; and I in turn flash the big-name-nearby signal to the other wives.

The most delectable coup of last season—and possibly of all time—was meeting Rock Hudson. He is nine feet tall and all of him gorgeous. Even Charles concurred that Rock is the most handsome man he ever saw. Realizing that Mr. H. must get terribly weary of gushing females, I opened our conversation with something sensible and offhand. "You *are* beautiful!" I said.

Then there was the time when we spied Elizabeth Taylor in the Italian restaurant we had chosen. The fact that her table was near the ladies' room caused such an unprecedented use of that facility, I'm sure the powder room attendant thought Maxine Gifford and I, among others, were victims of some terrible malady.

Our good friend, columnist Leonard Lyons, has contributed substantially in fattening my celebrity scalp belt. He frequently invites us to tag along as he covers his news beat, which includes the fancier supper clubs in New York, and good-naturedly sees to it that I get to shake the hand of every "anybody" in sight.

Several times a year team members are the guests of honor at post-game dinner-dances. In dancing with her husband's teammates, a wife is likely to discover that the Georgia Shuffle is not too different from the New Jersey Stomp, at that! John Lujack, who has assisted in telecasting the Giant games for the last few years, contends that the sociability of our group is, as he puts it, "largely responsible for the fact that the Giants have the best attitude of any team in the league. And a good attitude makes for good football." Johnny continues: "When I played for the Bears, as soon as a game was over the players scattered. Except for one or two couples we were especially fond of, we never saw each other outside the ball park. I'm convinced that getting to know all the men and their wives socially makes for better relations on the job. You guys really have it."

The congeniality of our group does much to compensate the Giant wives for their occasional weekends of "widowhood." Half of the games are played out of town, but rarely does the football wife travel with the team. Most Giant wives customarily make the Philadelphia trip (a distance of ninety miles). A few also follow the team to Washington. Seldom do we venture farther than that.

Several factors content us with staying behind. In the first place, the duration of each road trip is extremely short. Unlike the pro baseball player, whose schedule requires him to remain on the road for weeks at a time, the pro football player generally returns home between games, for he plays only once a week. (The West Coast teams provide the principal exception. Since Los Angeles and San Francisco are separated from the other NFL cities by a considerable distance, the Rams and 49ers find it expedient to remain in the East for a two-week stand on occasion.) In our case, the team usually flies out Saturday and returns on a chartered plane immediately after Sunday's game. So the husbands are gone and back almost before we have time to miss them.

The expense of traveling to distant league cities and the fact that Giant away games are televised in New York are two additional reasons the Giant wife does not mind forgoing the journey.

As soon as the menfolk are out of sight, phones begin to ring, and the hotel switchboard is jammed with What-time-do-we-leave? and What-are-you-going-to-wear? calls. I believe it was Pat Knight, former Giant halfback from San Antonio, who once told me: "You girls don't waste much time deciding how to spend your 'lonely' nights, do you?" I assumed an innocent expression as he continued. "When we were leaving for Pittsburgh last week, three of us stopped in the lobby and tried to call our wives because we had forgotten to tell them the name of the hotel we would be staying in. All three lines were busy! I finally asked the operator to break in, and Terry admitted she was checking on whether you all planned to eat dinner before or after the show. I believe you girls look forward to our leaving town!"

All I could think of to say was, "Aw, Pat." (And that is what I said.)

The husbands never seem to get accustomed to the idea that while they are away, we often sit up until daylight just talking. Sometimes these prolonged discussions follow a game of bridge or Scrabble or charades or Clue (a solve-the-murder game popular in our set for several seasons). Sometimes they result from a promise made by the wives who took in a play or a couple of movies to stop by and tell the "homebodies" about their evening on the town. We never mean to stay up all night; but there is something about the hours just before dawn which elicits a special frankness, an intimacy that tends to fade a little in strong sunlight.

The end of such meetings is generally precipitated by an incredulous gasp: "Oh my gosh! Do you know it's nearly five-thirty?" Thereupon each of us gathers up one of the sleeping children scattered about on beds or pallets and assists a multi-blessed mother with her transportation problems.

Charlie never ceases to be amazed at our intemperate hours. "What could you possibly find to talk about that long? You see each other every day!"

Men don't seem to understand that the more women see of each other, the more they have to talk about. We pool our remedies for thumb-sucking and bed-wetting, interfering mothers-in-law and soggy cornbread. We straighten out the world situation, tell jokes, change each others hair style (and/or color), and regale the group with stories about the home folks. I imagine the interesting people in Shellman, Georgia; or Kansas City; or Big Creek, Mississippi; or Bremerton, Washington; or Reidsville, North Carolina would be rather amazed to learn that the most fascinating of their exploits had been discussed at some length in far-off New York City!

Our Giant family has always been a closely knit unit. As in any sizable group, we naturally have our special friends and see more of them than we do of others. But the general relationship is extremely cordial. Perhaps it would be so without design; but rather than leave to chance anything so precious as team harmony, the elder wives engage in a certain amount of wholesome intrigue backstage.

Since so many of the married couples live in the same hotel, our principal efforts toward maintaining this congenial atmosphere take place here. When the new wives arrive, we of the old guard go calling to welcome them to the fold and to give them a list of pertinent phone numbers—our favorite grocer, pediatrician, gynecologist, theater ticket agency, drugstore, diaper service, and a laundry that almost always returns both socks.

We also tactfully drop hints about our organizational taboos—chief among them, the matters of thinking aloud and salary. We try subtly to impress on our rookie wives that since we all sit together at the games, no matter how excited a wife gets, she must not try to assess the blame for the failure of a play. Nor should she comment on a certain player's lapse. His wife might be sitting right behind her.

In my time we have had only one wife who wore her mouth on her sleeve. She was a most attractive girl who had an intelligent concept of the game. But in the heat of battle, she lost all sense of propriety. Whenever a Giant player erred noticeably, she invariably leaped to her feet shaking her fist and shouting epithets which were probably accurate but hardly born in sweetness and light. Unfortunately she was endowed with a very colorful vocabulary. Secret caucuses of the veteran wives produced complete agreement that something should be done, but persuading anyone to tie the bell around the cat's neck was another matter. In a cowardly fashion we voted to turn the problem over to Kyle Rote, whose position as co-captain of the team often involves duties more sensitive than tossing a coin before each kick-off. He diplomatically approached her husband, who perhaps not so diplomatically requested her to tone it down. At any rate she did, with the exception of a few well-chosen words directed at her own mate when *he* from time to time slipped below perfection on the playing field.

Post-game comments can be just as disquieting. If an unthinking wife finds fault with a player's performance, we elders try to turn it aside with something like, "You know, I don't know enough about the blocking assignments or the pass patterns to tell whose fault that was." It's an easy nine to five she doesn't either and is repeating, merely for the sake of conversation, a bit of misinformation she picked up from the intelligentsia in the standing-room crowd. In any event she usually realizes that we would rather talk about something else. And so would she, really.

Within our pigskin tower no mention is ever made of salary. I can think of no more effective way to blight a friendship than for a wife to know what another player earns. Betty Rote and I have been friends since the day we met. A person considered to be a true friend is generally someone who has served years of apprenticeship as an acquaintance. Somehow Betty and I skipped over the awkward stage and plunged directly into a friendship that has survived eleven years without a single minus. And yet I have no idea what Kyle's salary is; nor she Charlie's. And I wouldn't want to. Incidentally, to my knowledge Charlie's salary has never been accurately reported in print, and I must presume that estimates of other players' paychecks are also based on conjecture.

{12}

LIFE IN THE GRAND HOTEL

During the season the daily schedule of the football wife—while varying in minor detail from her normal routine in the hometown—is essentially the same. Washing and ironing and cooking are with her wherever she goes. But like women everywhere she manages to find time to compare notes with her peers. Due to the lack of a backyard fence, "clothesline conferences" are conducted on the way to the grocery, beside the sandpile in the park, and in one apartment or another.

The average transplanted wife, unaccustomed to hotel life, may find the confining atmosphere inconvenient where children are concerned. Park play must be closely supervised, and she cannot bundle the little ones off to Grandma's for the day whenever the notion strikes. Therefore, on completing her chores, she gathers up her brood and seeks the company of one or more wives also at liberty. Jointly they solve childhood's universal plaint ("Mama, I don't have anybody to play with!").

Sometimes the hotel wives baby-sit for each other. However, as Kathy Summerall puts it: "I am always

Charlie

Charlie

Charlie, Clarksdale
High School, 1940

Charlie in his baseball uniform during his Ole Miss years

Ole Miss freshman team: Doug Kenna, R. C. Britt, Charlie, Buddy Bowen, Ray Woodward, 1941 (Players were allowed to play only three years of varsity football in those days.)

Charlie, a Marine on Guam, World War II, 1944

Barney Poole, Coach
John Vaught, Charlie,
1947

Charlie, Ole Miss,
1947

Charlie and I at my junior prom a few weeks before he gave me my engagement ring, Mississippi State College for Women, Columbus, Mississippi, spring 1948

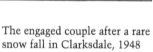

The engaged couple after a rare snow fall in Clarksdale, 1948

After the wedding . . . June 23, 1949

Giant Wives (kneeling): Betty (Kyle) Rote, Hazel (Jack) Stroud, Dianne (Ken) McAfee, Goodie (Bill) Austin, Carla (Herb) Rich; (back row), the QB wives: Barbara (Don) Heinrich, Perian (Charlie) Conerly, Judy (Bobby) Clatterbuck, early fifties

New York, New York! Frank Gifford, Eddie Arcaro, Toots Shor, Whitey Ford, Charlie, and Kyle Rote, mid-fifties

Eddie Price, Kyle Rote, Charlie, and Frank Gifford. Training camp, Bear Mountain, New York, 1954 or 1955.

Left to right: Charlie, Frank Gifford, Kyle Rote, Don Heinrich, and Pat Summerall

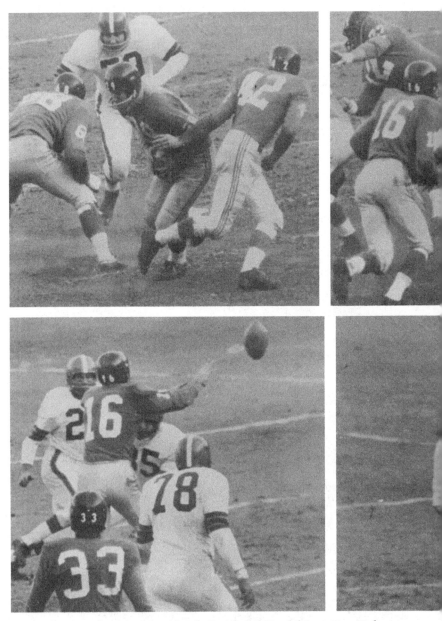

New York, December 21—Giants Razzle-Dazzle to a Touchdown—New York
Giants pull a double hand-off and lateral pass against Cleveland Browns for only
touchdown of NFL eastern division playoff game at Yankee Stadium today. As play
starts on Browns' 19-yard line, quarterback Charlie Conerly (42) hands off ball to

Alex Webster (29), who hands off ball to Frank Gifford (16). With a good block by Al Barry (68), Gifford breaks away to around the 12-yard line where he laterals ball to Conerly. Charlie is chased by Browns' Bob Gain (79), hit by Browns' Junior Wren (42), but falls across goal line.

Maxine and Frank Gifford
and Perian and Charlie,
1957

Charlie runs for his life, chased by Colts Art Donovan (70) and Gino
Marchetti (89), 1958

Trio of New York Giant backs (from left): Alex Webster, Charlie, and
Frank Gifford, who pulled the razzle-dazzle double-handoff-and-lateral for
the only touchdown of game against Cleveland Browns, pose with football
in dressing room after game December 21, 1958, in New York's Yankee
Stadium. New York won National Football League eastern division title
playoff, 10-0.

Charlie and offensive
coach Vince Lombardi
on the sidelines in
1956, the year the
Giants won the world
championship

Charlie Conerly Day
at Yankee Stadium,
November 29, 1959

Perian finally gets her Corvette. Conerly Day, Yankee Stadium,
November 29, 1959. Kyle Rote, Dumas Milner (the donor), Perian,
Charlie, and Andy Robustelli.

One of our Conerly Day gifts was a grand tour of Europe. Here we are in Paris, May 1960.

Archie Manning, Coach John Vaught, and Charlie, early sixties.

"The Marlboro Man" about town

Charlie: The Marlboro Man as a cowboy

At the Dinah Shore Tournament—30 years after this backfield won the NFL World Championship—1956 Giants: Alex Webster, Kyle Rote, Charlie, and Frank Gifford, 1986

For 20 years (1979–1999) our Quarterback group, including wives, gathered annually at exotic locations for golf and tons of fun. The 1986 team in Hawaii (bottom row, left to right): Don Meredith, Eddie LeBaron, Billy Kilmer, John Elway; (bottom middle row) Charlie, Doak Walker, Bobby Layne, Tobin Rote; (top middle row) Lynn Dickey, Craig Morton, Frank Gifford, Babe Parilli; (top row) Charley Johnson, Jim Hart, Sonny Jurgensen, Dan Fouts, Norm Snead, Ken Stabler, and John Hadl

Same people, different cake, our fortieth wedding anniversary

Charlie, still drawing applause from the New York crowd in 1993

a little leery of leaving my children for any length of time with another mother who has two or three of her own. I may venture as far as the grocery store after dropping Susie and Jay off to play, but no further. At that, my heart skips a beat whenever I hear a siren. You see, if the hotel were to catch fire while I was gone, I'm afraid I know whose children my 'sitter' would rescue first!"

The group engages more often in another form of mutual exchange: borrowing. Few of us can boast a complete set of kitchen utensils, for example, but everybody has something of value to lend. Beside the phone, there are lists of names and room numbers. And beside each is a notation:

Hazel—electric mixer.

Charlotte—big spaghetti pot.

Wanda—paprika; etc.

On the long practice days, four wives sometimes manage to consolidate the little nap-takers and play a hand or two of bridge before the men get home. Since, unfortunately, Charlie and I have no children, I was considered an automatic fourth until journalism began to intrude so rudely upon my leisure time.

Strolling down the hall one day en route to a bridge game, I encountered Adonis (Mrs. Jimmy) Patton with her ear pressed against the door of another wife's apartment— an intent, rather quizzical expression on her face. She started guiltily at my greeting; then admitted the obvious: "I'm eavesdropping," she explained. "And not a sound! I think Phyllis must hypnotize them. My boys have never been *this* quiet for so long. Every Saturday I expect her to have a *little* trouble with them—Russ bites, you know—and I feel I ought to be available just in case. But so far . . . I don't think she's in there."

"That's right," I interrupted. "Today *is* Sunday school day."

The confusion of each Sunday morning—game day—often prevents team parents from taking the little people to various and far-distant Sunday schools. Several years ago Phyllis Barry (wife of guard Al Barry) offered to remedy the situation by holding classes on Saturday mornings, but insisted that the mothers bow out after depositing their children in her apartment. It was outside her door we stood.

Just then the sweet, earnest strains of "Jesus Loves Me" wafted into the hall. Adonis and I fled in opposite directions. It is possible that her haste, like mine, was prompted by the wish to conceal a sudden foolish moistness of eye.

Holidays in the city do not hold quite the same luster as those spent at home. But Charlie and I rationalized long ago that, after all, home is where *we* are. We have spent only four Christmases in New York, for the regular season ends about the middle of December. We really didn't mind missing the festivities in Clarksdale on those occasions because our delay in returning home meant we had won the Eastern Conference title. The play-off game is customarily held a few days after Christmas, and who could ask for a better present than sharing in the glory and gilt of a World Championship contest?

The team children also have discovered that Santa Claus can find his way to the Bronx, and each Giant apartment is decorated with a shining tree in anticipation. Santa often leaves a note explaining that a few things (conveniently, the heaviest items like bikes) will be dropped off at Grandma's house back home so that she will be able to share a little belated Yuletide cheer with the grandchildren.

The wonderful friends we have made in New York over the years brighten our holidays with invitations to join their family circles.

On Thanksgiving the Giant owners either give each family a turkey or play host at a wholesale gathering of the clan to partake of the customary fixings. In either case, Charlie and I pace ourselves at noon because Toots and Baby Shor traditionally set a place for us at their table on Thanksgiving night. In addition to three lovely girls, the Shors have an apple-cheeked boy of eleven for whom Charles has a special fondness. Rory (called "Little Toots" outside the family) evidently returns this affection, for he calls Charlie "The Fearless Leader" and can describe in detail every pass Number 42 has completed in the last eight years. (He has a benevolent tendency to "disremember" the incompletions.) A Giant loss puts him to bed with a fever.

On Halloween the team fathers traditionally take the little people trick-or-treating. Armed with a list of room numbers, they guide the young goblins about the hotel. Last year's imaginative costumes included two Zorros, a flapper (complete with eye makeup and a "mink" stole), several clowns, more witches, and still more ghosts. At least half of the diminutive spooks were barely able to toddle. The kids were a little awed by their own spookiness. The event was enjoyed most by the mothers who dressed them and the fathers who showed them to the proper doors . . . and of course by door-openers like us, who nearly collapsed in sheer terror after each chorus of soft, hesitant "Boos!"

If hotel-life-with-children works a hardship in some ways on both parents and children, there are compensating factors. Teachers both in New York and at home have commented on the fact that well-traveled children are generally extremely well-adjusted. Though no more intelligent than others, they tend to be able to express themselves better, make new friends easily, and take new situations in stride. Indeed, how many non-traveled children of—say, six years—can operate a self-service elevator, order confidently in a restaurant, find the rest room on a train or plane without assistance, or keep room service attendants hopping while Mama naps?

Perhaps Life with the Little Pros can best be exemplified by the Rotes. Kyle and Betty are the proud, and sometimes bewildered, parents of three sons. Enterprise is the trademark of their eldest, who was born shortly before his father signed his initial contract with the New York Giants. Perhaps Kyle, Jr. inherited his flair for ingenuity from a distant ancestor, one Colorado Smith. (Mr. Smith holds the historically recorded distinction of being the last person clever enough to escape the Alamo alive.) Son Kyle, now twelve, not only plays football, as might be expected, but at the age of nine organized a suburban sandlot league, complete with regularly scheduled games. He was league commissioner, of course.

"Rookie," as his family and playmates prefer to call Kyle, Jr., has never been a child to sit idly by and wait to be entertained. During the time the Rotes lived in the Concourse Plaza Hotel, their Number One Son formed the Rote Errand Company. His clients: the Giant wives. For a five-cent service charge he would deliver mail to the rooms, purchase cigarettes in the lobby, borrow and return various cooking utensils, and even trot out for a loaf of bread. He was four and a half at the time.

Business being particularly slow one day, and without telling anyone, Kyle made an appointment with the hotel manager. He asked for a job. Unsuccessful but undiscouraged, Kyle proceeded to the newsstand in the lobby. He was hired on the spot, and worked off and on all season— straightening the displays and keeping the tender company. Much to the dismay of Mother Betty, his salary was customarily paid in Hershey bars. Another of Kyle, Jr.'s imaginative projects was nipped just beyond the bud by his horrified parents. Obtaining his father's autograph for his friends was one thing, but selling them in the park for ten cents apiece! . . .

Though it seems impossible, nine years have passed since Gary Rote joined the family. Looking back, I recall that the event was fraught with interesting byplay.

Forewarned that her second baby would be delivered by Caesarean section, Betty made the necessary advance arrangements with the doctor and the hospital. Since Kyle would be at practice during the specified check-in period (scheduled for the day preceding the operation) I agreed to accompany her instead.

That afternoon, suitcase in tow, Betty and I hailed a cab in front of the Concourse Plaza. It was soon evident that our driver previously had suffered at least one unfortunate experience concerning the urgency of ladies in delicate condition. Settled inside the taxi, I said innocently, "St. Vincent's Hospital, on Twelfth Street, please." (We were then on 161st.) The driver took one horrified look at Betty's ample form and shot from the curb with a desperate lurch. In half the time it normally takes, we careened the entire distance to the hospital—during the rush hour. On arrival, the semi-hysterical driver screeched to a double-parking halt and leaped out. Snatching up Betty's suitcase with one hand and Betty with the other, he bolted for the entrance. "Whew! Made it!" he exclaimed hoarsely as I paid the fare. Betty and I had been so engrossed in the exacting feat of preserving life and limb during the wild ride that neither of us had found the breath to tell him she wasn't in labor.

Things took a definite upturn the following day. Betty presented Kyle (and me) with a beautiful (he really was) seven-pound son.

It is typical of Gary Rote that so shortly after birth (even *before*—considering that cab ride) he should be instrumental in causing a certain amount of confusion. A few days before his fourth birthday the Rote's Number Two Son was responsible for an appalling bit of excitement in the Concourse Plaza. He contracted scarlet fever. (The doctor said he hadn't seen a case in years.) A careful count revealed that twenty-five people in the hotel had been exposed, including 80 percent of the Giant offensive team. It was just before the Pittsburgh game.

By eleven o'clock that night a frantic Betty Rote had finally notified the last contaminee and distributed pills prescribed by the doctor. All of us gulped mysterious white tablets for three days—still not clear about whether they would keep us from getting scarlet fever or merely keep us from dying when we did. Fortunately Gary's case proved to be a mild one—far less serious, in fact, than the damage to the nervous systems of the twenty-five pill-takers during that interminable incubation period.

"Fun with The Rotes" would not be complete without mentioning Christopher, a chubby cherub who at the age of eighteen months developed a mad passion for Auntie Peri. He became my constant shadow. It reached the point where Kyle and Betty had to spell my name in conversation. Otherwise, on hearing it spoken, Chris would set up a howl to pay me a visit—*regardless* of the hour. Once at 4 A.M. Betty rapped on our door, her squalling cherub under one arm. "I'm so sorry," she whispered, "but I figured it was better to wake just the two of you. Another few minutes of Chris's screaming is certain to rouse everyone in the hotel. He woke up a while ago,

Peri, and I made the mistake of telling him you would be mad if he didn't go right back to sleep . . . He wants to kiss you goodnight."

By design, the Rotes' apartment was customarily next to ours, an arrangement that fitted in handsomely with Christopher's one-track plans. From infancy, he exhibited signs of becoming a talented cat man. The tiny burglar would suddenly materialize in our apartment, having evidently walked right through two locked doors. At this tender age, Chris had a penchant (common to his ilk) for feeling soft material with two fingers of one hand while sucking the forefinger of the other. During most of his waking hours, Chris would cling to the hem of my garment indulging in his favorite pastime as I went about my household duties. I was inordinately flattered by such blind affection and adored every minute of it. Years passed before I would admit the truth to myself. Chris's overt devotion was due not to some inner radiance that shone from Aunt Peri, but to my customary "at home" attire—a housecoat made from extremely soft and cuddly material.

{13}

THE OBJECTIVE JOURNALIST

"Writing a letter?" Charlie threw his play book on the bed and glanced over my shoulder at a typewritten sheet marked "Page 3."

"No, the first of a series of articles for the *Clarksdale Press Register,*" I replied airily and absently, my mind groping for an elusive word.

"What in the world about?" He drew closer for a better look.

"Appalling!"

"A what?"

"Appalling. That's the word I've been trying to think of for thirty minutes. Oh—it's about professional football. At least the men who play it and their families."

"Why?"

"People seem to ask you the same type of questions every year when we get home. Well, the same thing happens to me, but they ask instead about how we live, the wives, children, New York. Things like that. So I decided to write a column once a week and tell them what goes on . . . Here . . . read it and see what you think."

Silence.

"There are a few salient observations about last week's game," I add, "and some locker-room gossip I picked up from Don Heinrich I'd like you to check."

He checks. "Sounds fine, but what does meeting Ernest Hemingway and seeing *Auntie Mame* have to do with football? To say nothing of Gary Rote's scarlet fever . . ."

"Well, nothing really. But women are interested in that side of our life with football. By including something for everybody, I hope to entice the whole family to read it. That is, if the paper prints it!"

I mailed the first installment of "Backseat Quarterback" to Joe Ellis, editor of the *Clarksdale Press Register* (circulation 4400), making it plain I expected to be paid should he decide to use the articles. Three days later I received a wire from Joe. "Keep them coming," he said. "Mail in time for Saturday publication." And so began my professional literary career.

The next summer (1958), I approached Mr. Purser Hewitt, editor of the *Jackson (Mississippi) Clarion-Ledger-News* (circulation 76,000) and convinced him that the C.-L.-N. should also carry "Backseat Quarterback." He agreed to run the column on Sundays so as not to scoop the *Press Register* (published every evening except Sunday), since some people in Clarksdale subscribe to both papers. Now, mildly syndicated, I contacted other papers throughout the mid-South, but was not as fortunate. In fact, the series met with total rejection.

The next year, two national magazines, intrigued with the notion of a woman sports writer, ran brief stories about my "career," both including quotes from articles I had written. As a result, John Wheeler, guiding light of the North American Newspaper Alliance, phoned and requested a conference to explore the possibility of syndicating my material through his organization. After reading several of the "Backseat Quarterback" clippings Mr. Wheeler mumbled something vaguely complimentary, but I could see that "Don't-call-me" look in his eyes. I quickly whipped from my purse an article I had written "just for instance" about men who impersonate pro football players for fun and profit, and blurted: "I expect the columns written for our home state are a little too local. Here is an article of more general interest that might be more suitable for national distribution."

He read the typewritten copy carefully and tossed it onto his desk. "Yes, this is what we want. Have another one in by Thursday."

Thus I became not only mildly, but also genuinely syndicated.

I have always liked to write, but soon discovered that *having* to write was something else again. The dark cloud of the deadline, dormant since the days with the college newspaper, reasserted itself. The chatty, diary-type column written for home state consumption has never posed a serious problem. Though it requires a certain amount of time, there is never a dearth of material. Coffee with one or another of the well-informed wives is usually sufficient to provide the necessary information about current hotel activities. The portion devoted to football itself is based on conversations with Charles and/or several of my voluble player-friends.

Composing an article after a win turned out to be infinitely more enjoyable than after a defeat.

The time devoted to my three projects (the two columns and this book) combined to make 1961 a rather untypical year, socially. I had to learn to put aside the temptation of bouncing from one apartment to another each morning for girl talk. In years past I often rushed out the door before the morning dishwater had time to gurgle down the drain.

I always try to complete as much of the actual writing as possible while Charlie is at practice so I won't overdo the career wife role in his presence. Though he seems proud of my journalistic efforts, I don't believe Charlie has ever quite gotten used to the fact that anyone would actually pay money for them. For that matter, neither have I.

As any writer can attest, there is a certain sly satisfaction engendered by seeing oneself in print. When the Clarksdale paper first began to run my articles back in 1957, four weeks went by before I saw a copy. Letters from home made frequent mention of the series, but everyone thought everyone else was sending me the clippings. Charles could not understand my frustration. "You wrote them—why are you so anxious to read them?" he said.

Accumulating a bit of mad money was a pleasing side effect of writing professionally. It had always seemed a little ludicrous to buy Charlie a birthday or Christmas present—and then charge it to him! For the first time in my life I was independently wealthy.

As a buffer against the uncertainties of the future, I had made certain that my college diploma was accompanied by a teacher's license. But the six-week practice-teaching stint which was among the requirements for obtaining it underlined the suspicion that perhaps my talents lie elsewhere. My class in senior English was composed primarily of Columbus High football players. These perceptive youths, well aware that I was engaged to Charlie at the time, were surprisingly adept at converting a discussion of the split infinitive into one about the Split-T! There is little question that I probably knew as much (or as little) about one as the other; and the experience convinced me that, for the sake of the citizens of tomorrow, it is just as well that the license gathers dust in our safety deposit box at the Coahoma County Bank.

I have reaped another benefit from sports writing. In gathering information for the columns by interviewing players about various phases of the game, I have learned a great deal about football. In fact, I now know about half as much as people assume I do.

For instance, in recent years Giant quarterbacks, along with others, have employed with success what they call "automatics"—changing the planned play at the line of scrimmage. As the teams line up for the snap, Charlie may see that the defense is set up to defeat the play he had just called in the huddle. He then redirects the action to their weak side by substituting at the last minute a more advantageous play.

Now that's all tricky and fine. But one thing had always bothered me: Since he must speak loudly enough for his own men to hear the change in strategy, what's to prevent the opponents inches away from eavesdropping?

I posed the question to Charlie, who replied patiently: "At the line of scrimmage I always call out a play just before the ball is snapped. In ordinary circumstances it is a dummy play which our offensive men disregard because they have already gotten their real instructions in the huddle. Now—if I want to change those instructions, I throw in a key number. This 'secret word' alerts them to the fact that I'm switching signals, and the play I am about to call is the one we will actually run. Of course the defenders also hear the call, but they can't tell the difference between the usual dummy play and an 'automatic' substitution."

Simple? He says so.

Giant place-kicker Pat Summerall is one of my prime sources of information. Hardly a week passes that I don't intrude on his and wife Kathy's leisure time by arriving at the Summerall apartment, note pad in hand. (Pat's ability to explain things clearly to the juvenile mind is put to work during the off-season too. He holds a master's degree and for several years has taught American history at the Lake City, Florida, high school.)

On one occasion, I was curious about the importance (if any) of the holder, the man who holds the ball for the kicker. I noticed that even though Charlie may be out of the game due to reasons of strategy or poor health, when a place-kicking situation arises, the quarterback playing retires. And if Charles is able to limp from the bench to the line of scrimmage, he comes in to hold for Summerall's field goal and extra-point attempts—as he did for Ray Poole and Ben Agajanian before Pat. Since it thus seems important to Pat (and to kickers on other NFL teams) to have the same holder each time, I asked him why. Superstition? Habit?

"Neither," replied Pat. "I insist that Charlie hold if he is physically able for several reasons. He gets the ball down quicker for one thing. And he always puts it on the spot. If you'll notice, before each kick I make a mark on the turf with my cleats to indicate where I want him to set it down. And I know it will always be right there. Charlie also spins the ball so that I never have to kick the laces— an eccentricity of mine, but one that is essential to me. Most important of all, I have confidence in Charlie. The entire operation, from center snap to kick, takes only two seconds, so you see the job requires someone who knows what he is doing." It is typical of Pat that he made the holder sound more important than the kicker.

This conversation led to a discussion of the role of the center—that long-suffering lineman who rarely gets his name in the paper unless he lobs the ball over the head of the holder or punter. By now Charlie had joined our group to wax enthusiastic about Giant center Ray Wietecha. "The best in the league," he exclaimed. "Ray socks that ball into my hands with the same degree of firmness and rhythm each time." And his ability to center the ball 'blind' gives us an extra man in the offensive line."

Pat noticed my wondering look and explained: "Many centers find their accuracy is impaired unless they keep their eyes on the ball. However, by the time they complete the snap and look up, the line charge is underway. Consequently they may be of little value in assisting the offensive strategy. Kind of a Where-did-everybody-go? situation. Ray has the feel of his job so memorized that he is able to snap the ball with his head *up*. He's able to swing into action the instant everyone else does . . ."

Charlie broke in. "Even on the punt formation snap"— he paused, and I nodded to indicate that I understood in this case the ball travels about fifteen yards—"Ray can judge the proper distance without looking."

While I had Pat and Charlie cornered, I brought up another puzzling aspect of pro football. "Just how much harm can a player who is traded from one team to another do by 'informing' on his former teammates? It seems to me that he could give his current coaches a lot of valuable information about his old team. In fact he could tip them off about every play in his former book . . ."

Charlie answered that one. "Usually the only worthwhile information that changes hands concerns personnel, but it's seldom something we don't already know. Because of films and scouts and actual experience, there are few secrets in this league. It becomes merely a matter of guessing when the other team will do what. But execution is what's important. You don't fool 'em—you *beat* 'em."

One night after supper I began to solicit a little pertinent information from Charlie. We were still sitting at the table, and I had shoved the dishes aside to make room for my note pad. As he clarified each point, I would jot down the result (using my private system of shorthand) and systematically ask another question.

Suddenly I burst out laughing. Charles, seeing nothing particularly amusing about the strategy behind an onside kick, was mildly startled. "What's the matter?"

"Nothing, really," I said. "I was just thinking that a stranger who happened on this little scene would have no idea that we even knew each other. We're both being so business-like." And indeed we had been so submerged in the roles of interviewer and interviewee it was as if I were the standard inquiring reporter quizzing an athlete I knew by reputation only.

That consultation had been prompted by a disappointment handed us by Washington in the previous week's game. Late in the fourth quarter the Giants were leading by two touchdowns. What happened in the dying moments is the reason that veteran spectators of pro football do not leave their seats until the final gun.

Outplayed all day, the Redskins suddenly caught fire and scored, closing the gap to one touchdown. It was apparent to both teams that the only way the Redskins could hope to score again with two minutes remaining would be to get their hands on the ball *immediately*. And that the only way they could hope to accomplish this was through the use of a desperation maneuver that succeeds only rarely—the short kick. The standard field-spanning kick-off would avail them nothing. One series of clock-killing plays by the receiving Giants and the game would be over.

The Redskin kicker lined up and ran at the ball forcefully, as if to send it far downfield. Instead, he checked his pace a step before he made contact and kicked it gently—but not too gently. As he had hoped, his "onside kick" was too hot to handle. The ball took a skidding bounce, struck Giant safetyman Jimmy Patton in the chest, popped straight up, and fell into the arms of an onrushing Redskin. (Here Charlie emphasized that Jimmy could not be charged with a fumble because he never had his hands on the ball.) Unlike a punt, which belongs to the receivers even if they allow it to roll dead, a kick-off must be fielded (brought under control) by the receiving team. If the ball travels at least ten yards, it becomes the property of either team on a first-come, first-served basis.

The Redskin maneuver was not a masterful stroke of strategy that caught the Giants napping. In anticipation of the short kick, Coach Jim Lee Howell had stationed two of our best defensive ball hawks up front—Patton and Dick Lynch, one in each corner. Despite this precaution, the Redskins impolitely took the first serving. And, in possession of the ball at midfield, the inspired Washington team went on to tie the score.

In addition to enhancing my football education, the unlikely role as a sports reporter affords me the opportunity of refuting in print many popular misconceptions. These stem from the fact that football is probably the most complicated of all sports—and therefore the most difficult to understand. The average fan is obviously endowed with sufficient knowledge of the game to enable him to exact an enormous amount of pleasure from it. But it is almost impossible for him to comprehend *all* its complexities unless he has actually played the sport—if only on the neighborhood sandlots. I said "almost." There are exceptions, and I am definitely not one of them! I have lived with pro football for thirteen years, but invariably get lost when the third "O" brush-blocks the "X" on his left and sprints down the blackboard.

Being closer to the game and to the men who play it, it is only natural that I am keenly aware of the unfair judgments sometimes handed down by the "grandstand officials" who understand the situations they see only in part. (This is particularly unsettling when an unflattering comment is directed audibly at the husband of the Giant wife in the next seat.) Players are human. They make mistakes. What a dull game it would be if they did not. It is blame *unfairly* assessed that leads me to the soapbox.

Take, for example, the moans of disgust that often follow the fair-catch signal given by a safety man in no apparent danger of immediate inundation. "Why, he could have made ten yards before they got to him. That kid just doesn't like to be tackled," the man across the aisle confides to his wife and nearby fans.

In the first place, there is not a single player of my acquaintance who *does* enjoy being tackled. But I digress. There are usually two men back to field the punt. As it approaches, they chat, as baseball outfielders do, about which one is in the best position to make the catch. A second decision is necessary, especially in the event of a high punt. It would be very difficult for the receiver to keep his eye on the ball and at the same time to estimate the speed of the oncoming defenders. The latter duty is undertaken by the "idle" safety man. It is he who decides whether his partner will have time to gain control of the ball and make yardage, or whether the opponents are too close and will likely smear him immediately, causing a possible fumble.

Take into consideration, too, that once the defensive men see the fair-catch signal, they automatically slow pace to avoid making contact and incurring an automatic penalty. (Once the waiting receiver has made the fair-catch signal, he's made a contract. He agrees to field the ball and not attempt to make any yardage. The onrushing enemy agrees, by the rules of the game, not to tackle him.) Thus it sometimes appears that the receiver has more leisure time than he would have had if his opponents had not pulled in the reins.

On certain occasions—notably when the ball is wet, or freezing weather causes numb fingers—the safety men receive instructions from the bench to fair-catch *every* punt as a precaution against muffs or fumbles.

An angry yowl usually rises from the stands when a mammoth lineman bangs into a ballcarrier already downed or in the process of being put down by an adversary. "Dirty player," the gentleman across the way mumbles. "He's piling on to try to knock the runner out of the game." I wonder if the mumbler ever paused to reflect upon the difficulty a 260-pound man running full tilt has in stopping on a dime?

And what of the pass defender who is made to appear a trifle foolish when the ball is hauled in for long yardage just as he races up? "Why do they keep that guy? He's asleep at the switch again," laments the aisle-sitter. It is just possible that the defender in question had completed his duties on one side of the field. Then, noting that the man responsible for protecting the other zone had been taken out of the play, he raced to the opposite side of the field in a vain attempt to undertake his teammate's assignment. Such intricate situations escape an offensive-minded spectator like me—until after the game. It is then I overhear the man initially responsible for making the defense laud the "sleepwalker" for a brilliant (though futile) effort.

Pass interference, real and imagined, is a play involving judgment and is frequently misunderstood by spectators—and understandably so. Many players bear the brunt of grandstand displeasure when they collide with a would-be receiver. But to give the devil his due: *During a forward pass it must be remembered that defensive players have as much right on the path to the ball as eligible opponents. Any bodily contact, however severe, between players who are making a bona fide and simultaneous attempt to catch or bat the ball is not interference. . . .* The preceding partial explanation is from one of the more lucid passages in the official NFL Rule Book, which in some instances makes Einstein's Theory of Relativity look like the second-grade "Think and Do" workbook. (End of report from the Grievance Committee.)

Charlie assists in my writing career at more than the dinner table. Every few weeks I prepare a questionnaire which he obligingly takes along to practice sessions at the Stadium. Not wishing to make a nuisance of myself, I suggest each time that he merely post the list of questions in a prominent spot. Instead, he polls the players individually in order to secure the information and/or opinions requested. "If I just tacked it up on the bulletin board, I doubt if they would pay any attention to it," he explains.

Besides being my "leg man," Charlie reads everything I write for publication and checks it for technical accuracy and careless error. For instance, I have a bad habit of using "Pittsburgh" and "Philadelphia" interchangeably. There are those who object. Sometimes I hark back to the olden days by mistakenly using the name of a former Giant who for some reason reminds me of the current player I am writing about. I also occasionally have tackles doing the things guards do and vice versa.

Charlie functions as a consultant, but I draw the line at spousely censorship. He regards any explanation of misfortune as an outright alibi. If I allowed him to delete all such "clarifications" from hometown articles following Giant defeats, very often there would be nothing left but my by-line.

Charlie is extremely patient in answering stupid questions and explaining elementals—as long as I don't immobilize him too long. However, seldom does he *volunteer* information (as my more professional colleagues in sportswriting can verify).

Kyle Rote, among other helpers, is different. He not only furnishes the facts I request, but on several occasions began a phone conversation with the suggestion: "Peri, this week why don't you write about . . ." You might imagine that a man so thoughtful of others would enjoy a certain measure of popularity. Such an assumption would be valid. Seven of his teammates have shown their admiration for Kyle by naming sons after him. (Patton, Gifford, Heinrich, Triplett, Summerall, and Beck of the Giants; and Collier, a classmate at SMU).

Former Giant quarterback Don Heinrich became my locker room spy. Don returned to the fold as backfield coach after a year with the Dallas Cowboys. During his absence my articles suffered from a distinct scarcity of insignificant but humorous incidents that make good reading.

Much of my information comes from eavesdropping— which frequently causes Charlie and his fellows to pause suddenly in the midst of an "inside" story, shoot an apprehensive glance in my direction, and chuckle half-seriously, "Peri, this is off the record, of course."

Journalism has still another fringe benefit. As far as I know, I am the only female member of the Football Writers Association of America. A member in name only, perhaps; I don't really *do* anything; but I take great pleasure in flashing my press card before impressionable dinner companions. And if things get dull around the house, I tease Charlie by noisily making plans to attend the annual FWAA convention in Chicago. "So sorry you can't go too," I console him, "but our meeting coincides with the College All-Star game, and you'll be in training camp."

Such balderdash doesn't disturb him, but he is mildly disconcerted by the fact that mail from the organization is addressed to *Mr.* Perian Conerly. (Confusion about the gender of my first name is understandable. The spelling does not indicate that it is pronounced Perry Ann, being a contraction of two family names.)

Charlie did emit a groan, too, when the first All-America ballot arrived from the FWAA and I sat down to cast my vote for that year's perfect college team. As it happened—having rather lost touch with "amateur" football—I tore up my ballot when he pointed out that ten of the eleven men I had selected for the All-America honor played for Ole Miss.

{14}

HOW TO AVOID FIGURING IN THE ODDS

"Gonna win next Sunday?"

Every football player in the professional leagues hears this query a dozen times a week. Generally it is a rhetorical question offered in the same detached spirit as "How's the family?" Even so, though he realizes that this is usually an attempt at making polite conversation, a player must choose his words carefully in reply—and even be wary of tone of voice. No one expects him to say that his team will *lose* its next game. Yet he cannot afford to be overly optimistic either. Undue enthusiasm might be interpreted as some kind of green light. Charlie's stock answer is typically noncommittal: "Well, I surely hope we can beat them."

Even the players' wives must present their views on the subject vaguely; for, as I was astounded to learn several years ago, there are people who actually think we "know something." I have always been eager to talk football with almost anyone who will listen. (In fact, it is

Charlie's considered opinion that I am willing to talk to anyone about anything, but that is neither here nor there.) Even before realizing that my inconsequential notions might be taken seriously, I am always careful to preface any discussion with a hackneyed but completely accurate paraphrase: "The opinions about to be expressed here are not necessarily those of my husband." I also belabor the obvious by pointing out that there are a few (thousand) things about the game that I do not fully understand. Then I customarily round out the foreword by revealing that I am a confirmed optimist. Having established this background, I am ready to enter into an enthusiastic discussion of our way of life.

But on one occasion I was jolted by the realization that one man, inordinately curious about the possible outcome of a game, might act on what I was saying. I began to suspect that, despite the forewarnings, he was harboring the ridiculous intention of *betting* in accordance with my views. Nervously I groped for a change of subject, finally bursting into a disjointed monologue about the antics of our team children. Somehow he managed to steer the conversation back to the approaching game. I interrupted frantically with another kiddie story. Suddenly he applied the *coup de grâce:* "The morning line is 3½. What do you think?"

Gulping several times, I reiterated that my information was about as "inside" as the outside page of the sports section. I cautioned the silly fellow that even my intuition is distorted by desire: I predict the Giants will win by at least

35–0 *every* time they take the field. Then I bade him a hasty good night and repaired to the ladies' room to mop the cold sweat from my brow. Nowadays I turn aside any suspicious reference to a specific game with some original statement. "Well, I surely hope we can beat them," for example.

Most people don't try to seek definite opinions from the players themselves, but occasionally an unthinking soul will persevere. Charlie once told a persistent man who wouldn't let the matter drop: "Look, fellow. I just met you. If I *did* 'know something'—and I don't—it stands to reason that I wouldn't tell *you*. If I ever got hold of the kind of information you're talking about and was foolish enough to try to use it, I believe I could find someone a little closer to home to share the benefits with. Now either change the subject or shove off."

"Uncomfortable" might describe Charlie's condition after a question like that. "Irritated!" would be a better description of his mood when assailed with the sad story of someone who has lost money by betting on the Giants. I remember Charlie's softly-turned reply to an acquaintance who moaned that he had lost a wager because the Giants failed to "cover the point spread"—that is, didn't win by as large a margin as they were "supposed" to. Charlie immobilized the fellow with a cold glare. "We're paid to win football games, friend—not bets."

Naturally, any team wants to make as handsome a showing as possible. Professional athletes are men of pride. On the other hand, their principal concern is victory, not margin of victory. I am reminded of another game, one played in New York. The Giants, leading by three points, were in possession near the opponents' thirty-yard line. The next play would be the last of the game. As Charles snuggled the ball in place in order to run out the clock, a chorus of booing rang from the stands. The cries of discontent almost drowned out the final gun.

"I was puzzled," recalls Charlie. "My first thought was that there were an awful lot of out-of-town rooters in the crowd. When I got back to the dressing room, I said, 'What were they booing about? We won, didn't we?'"

One of the trainers answered: "The Giants were favored by *four* points. The bettors wanted Summerall sent in to try for a field goal."

"And risk having them block it and maybe beat us by running it back for a touchdown—when we had the game already won?" Charles's tone of incredulity sufficed to explain why the vociferous wagerers were not accommodated.

A peace-loving soul by nature, I cringe every time a foolhardy cabdriver turns to the several healthy players in the back seat and snorts, "What *happened* to you guys last Sunday? I lost twenty bucks on that game."

Charlie is relatively even-tempered. But one day some of his more choleric colleagues might react to a complaint of that nature with something stronger than a verbal squelch—particularly should it follow too closely on the heels of a painful defeat. It might be reasonable to assume that in most cases the player lost a great deal more than did the tactless bettor (via chances for the championship purse, fees from endorsements and personal appearances, and a frailer basis for next year's salary talks, not to mention injured pride). In addition, he just might have lost a few teeth and be in the mood to even the score. So if anyone of your acquaintance has a proclivity for wagering on the outcome of football games, you might be doing him a toothsome favor to suggest that he refrain from detailing his financial reverses in the presence of those directly concerned.

Seriously, I suppose that many of the people who make a point of telling players about their losses are true fans who are merely attempting to prove their loyalty by revealing their willingness to lay their confidence on the (morning) line. However, you can imagine that the usual sums mentioned by average bettors might sound humdrum to a player who has just seen five thousand dollars in championship money slip through his fingers in the course of one dismal afternoon.

Confronting a player with news of a bet *won* on his team makes him just as nervous (though perhaps not as angry). He would just as soon forget there are such things as odds and point spreads and morning lines. However, since almost every newspaper in the country takes careful note of their existence, the best he can do is try to ignore them.

Shocked by the 1946 attempt to fix a professional football game, the National Football League instituted various precautions to prevent a recurrence of that besmirching. Operatives in league cities and other population centers move quietly in the sphere of the gambling element. Should the theoretical odds take a sudden, inexplicable swerve in either direction these men act quickly to find out why. Most often they discover that the sudden change of heart is dictated by news of a key injury on one of the teams.

NFL coaches are directed to make injury lists a matter of public record immediately. Until enlightened, I argued that for reasons of strategy it might be wise for a team to conceal vital injuries from its upcoming opponents. I was told that past experience has proved such attempts are futile and would merely encourage an inter-team espionage system.

There is a less clearly defined motive for this free exchange of information. Although football moguls can ill afford to exhibit any interest whatsoever in the foibles of the gaming public, they realize that concealing injuries would work a hardship on the small bettor. The professional gambler would undoubtedly go to great lengths to uncover even the best-kept secret. The "little man," not having access to such information, would be at a disadvantage.

At the risk of lifetime disbarment from football, players are instructed to report to their coaches or team owners any bribe offer or suspicious conversation. They are also warned against associating with known gamblers. Even an innocent chance meeting could set the grapevine abuzzing with sinister interpretations.

I still erupt in a mild case of hives when remembering an incident which happened several years ago in a

New York restaurant. Frank Gifford and I were still in the midst of our entrees while Charles, a notably swift eater, was sipping his after-dinner coffee. An acquaintance appeared at the table. "If you're through eating, Charlie, I wonder if you'd mind coming over to meet my wife. She's been bugging me all evening."

Charles complied. There were several others in the party, and after exchanging How-do-you-dos, Charlie refused their invitation to sit down, saying: "Giff has to leave in a few minutes, so I'd better get back to my wife."

Later the acquaintance rejoined us, looking a trifle distraught. "Charlie, I want to apologize. I just wasn't thinking! A man in my profession meets all kind of people. In spite of everything, this guy is really good company. And he *is* retired."

Charlie looked up, puzzled.

"Don't you know who that was? The older fellow, I mean?"

"No, I didn't catch his name."

"That was ——" (mentioning a character reputedly in charge of a syndicate's gambling operation for many years).

Charlie almost forgot to pay the bill in his haste to vacate the premises.

{15}

FIGHTING

A question frequently asked of Charles by reporters attempting to spice up a routine interview concerns "dirty" football players. Not adverse to a little spice myself occasionally, I asked him one day to expound.

"Naturally there are a few rotten apples in *any* barrel," he began warily, "but most players have the decency and good sense to avoid purposely injuring a man. We all realize that football is a means of livelihood for us. The live-and-let-live rule applies . . ."

"You sound like Bartlett's Quotations," I said, needling. "How sweet."

"Now this has nothing to do with good hard football. It's a rough game and players are taught to hit hard. But they aren't trying to kill anybody. Their assignment is to knock the opponents out of each play as it develops—not out of the game entirely. Of course there are exceptions."

"Yes?"

"But the men who resort to dirty tactics are generally second-rate. A top-notch player doesn't have to. He's skillful enough to complete his assignment legally.

"Besides, even the bad actors have sense enough to know that they can't get by forever with the dirty stuff. Remember, we play every team in our conference twice a season—and there is always next year. A guy who's too handy with the elbows and knees will find sooner or later that his opponents also have two of each."

"How does this work?" I asked, ignorantly but not innocently.

"If he gets too rough too often, he'll discover that his victim has ten friends on the field. There's always the bootsie."

Charles was referring to a punitive measure. Actually it is rarely used, but the fact that it *might* be serves as deterrent. The bootsie play usually is called on to correct the bad manners of a player who has deliberately injured another. Opponents of the willful disabler discuss the matter in the huddle. Should their team be on offense, one player is assigned to snuggle the ball in place, making no attempt to advance it. At the snap, all other players rush at the offender. Those who succeed in reaching him dispense a little of his own medicine.

Since the bootsie does not exactly typify the precept of turning the other cheek, players are reluctant to admit its existence. The only concrete instance I could dredge up concerns a bootsie that didn't quite come about. The incident occurred during Emlen Tunnell's heyday as the league's most feared safety man. In one game Em was performing his specialties to perfection. He made several significant run-backs, intercepted two passes, and his jarring tackles were the hit of the grandstands. Perhaps this show of excellence accounted for the fact that a huge opposing end was out to get Em.

Since both the cat and the mouse were members of their teams' defensive units, the only time they were on the field at the same time was during punts and kick-offs. The pugnacious end made the most of these opportunities; whether actually receiving the ball or not, Em found himself on the wrong end of an unfriendly knee as each play culminated. The sinewy little safety brushed aside the concern of his teammates with a determined "I can take care of myself." But finally he absorbed a blow that left him on the ground unconscious.

Now, Em was a special favorite among his fellows; and when the Giant offensive team assembled for the next play, irate whispers of "Bootsie! Bootsie!" echoed through the huddle.

"Bootsie," decreed Charlie.

Not wishing to reveal their intention by breaking from the huddle too soon, the players held their positions a few seconds longer than usual. During this instant cooler thinking prevailed, and the other old heads nodded their approval of Charlie's change of heart: "Look, fellows, the game is almost over, and we might mess around here and lose it. Check the bootsie. We play these guys again in a couple of weeks. Let's wait till then. Repeat: Check the bootsie." And he called quickly for a fullback dive.

However, halfback Frank Gifford, who was to be set out as a flanker on the initial call, was already in the process of assuming his split position when the change was announced and therefore was not aware that the bootsie was off. At the snap he rushed forward and banged the bad boy to the ground. It would be difficult to say who was more surprised—Frank, who waited in vain for help from his teammates (not that he needed it), or the object of his disaffection, who was shocked into momentary inactivity by this unexpected attack from a player so much smaller than he. Fortunately for Frank, an observant official nearby parted the two before the bully recovered his aplomb. Incidentally, either an understanding coach or a convenient injury kept the wary end on the bench during the next encounter between the two teams.

Coaches and game officials alike frown on such tactics; but oddly enough, the teammates of a bootsied man seldom offer strenuous objection. A dirty player is a detriment to his own team. His actions invariably result in loss of valuable yardage via unnecessary roughness penalties. A man with a bad reputation comes under close scrutiny from the officials. Even a borderline action by him will be construed as malice, whereas a comparable act committed by a player of good repute may draw only a warning.

In days gone by, the Giants employed a tremendous lineman who furnished an exception to the assumption that only mediocre players are dirty. He was among the best in the league. Unfortunately the man had a Jekyll-and-Hyde personality. Off the field he was a shy, mild-mannered individual, one of the gentlest people I have ever known. On the field he was possibly the roughest

I have ever seen. His favorite illegal act was holding, but frequently he was called down for delivering a decisive blow to an opponent. His participation in a game was tantamount to spotting an opposing team anywhere from thirty to sixty yards, and not a Sunday passed that he did not incur at least two fifteen-yard penalties. Pro teams are too evenly matched to escape the consequences of giving an opponent such consistent advantage.

Charlie added to my small store of knowledge: "Since football is a contact sport, I guess almost every player has gotten mad enough to fight at some time or other. And naturally some men are more hot-tempered than others. But there is a difference between losing your temper and deliberately setting out to hurt somebody."

"Kind of like comparing temporary insanity with cold-blooded murder?" I injected helpfully.

"Exactly. Now I'm not a fighter, myself. In the first place I've got good eyes," he grinned. "At least good enough to tell when a man outweighs me some eighty or ninety pounds. And in the second, I learned a long time ago that nobody ever really wins a fight. I had my last real fight when I was fifteen—in a parking lot full of cinders. When it was over, the other boy and I both had bloody noses and scratches and our clothes were all torn. We shook hands and sat down together to figure out how we were going to explain things to our parents."

"How about that little encounter in the Cardinal game six or seven years ago?" I reminded him of the only time in his long career that he had been thrown out of a game.

Charles had interpreted a stinging blow administered by the elbow of a large Chicago end as a deliberate attempt to incapacitate. He replied in kind, and the two tussled briefly on the ground before the referee sent both to the bench.

Charlie smiled sheepishly. "I figured somebody would stop us before I hurt him *too* badly! . . . But, seriously, remember when he came over after the game and apologized? He told me it really was an accident because he didn't make enough money to risk wasting it paying fines. [The NFL imposes an automatic fine of fifty dollars upon players who are ejected from a league game by the officials.] He was telling the truth. I apologized too."

"Remember? When he came running up to you after the game, I thought at first he was ready to continue the proceedings. I was frantic because by then all the officials were heading for the locker room, and the few Giant players remaining on the field weren't paying any attention. I knew you'd need all the help you could get!"

"Well, I must admit I put my helmet back on when I saw him coming toward me. By the way, that's the first rule of fighting on the football field. When it looks as if trouble is brewing—even if you're on the bench—FIND A HELMET AND PUT IT ON!"

"I'm chicken. Let's talk about Frank's last injury," I prompted. "You were mad enough to fight that day." I was referring to the serious concussion which influenced Frank Gifford's temporary retirement from football. (On advice of his doctor, Frank sat out the 1961 season, but signed up to play again in 1962.) Giff was not only our star halfback, but also one of Charlie's best friends and his training camp roommate.

Charlie obliged: "Well, as you know, we were playing the Eagles that day and still had a good chance to overhaul them in the race for the Eastern Conference title. I was out of action with a bad knee, watching from the bench while George Shaw guided the team toward what might possibly have been the tying score. He called Giff's pass number. Frank caught the ball easily and steamed around right end for the first down. Just then Chuck Bednarik [an Eagle linebacker] slammed into him from the blind side. Frank was knocked unconscious and naturally lost the ball. The Eagles recovered. That was the ball game.

"What burned me up was the fact that Bednarik did a little jig while Frank was just lying there. Why, I thought he might be dead! When I cooled off a little, I realized that Chuck was so happy because the Eagles had recovered the fumble and ended our drive. But at the time he seemed to be laughing and pointing because he had hurt Frank. As it turned out, I think the doctors decided that the concussion was caused by the way Frank hit the ground and not by the shock of the tackle itself. And Giff says it was a clean tackle, so I guess it was."

In concluding our interview, Charles had one last wry comment concerning gridiron pugilism: "If you've just got to fight, you'd better be the one to start it—because the fellow who lands the counterpunch is always the one the referee catches in the act and throws out of the game."

{16}

PHYSICAL UNFITNESS

Physical fitness is a prerequisite for the professional athlete. Or is it? The National Football League is rampant with top-flight players whose talent and desire have overcome seemingly overwhelming physical handicaps.

Ray Berry, Baltimore's scintillating end, is perhaps the most outstanding example of a man who ignored the fact that he is a triple-threat "physical wreck" to become one of the league's all-time greats. Contact lenses aid his faulty vision. One of Ray's legs is shorter than the other. No problem. Ray simply dons a shoe fitted with thickened cleats to compensate for the difference. A malformation of the back sometimes causes his sacroiliac to lock and prevent him from straightening up. With a gentle twist by the trainer to snap it back into place, Ray is ready to catch another touchdown pass.

The effectiveness of "Bootin' Ben" Agajanian, who served as Giant field goal and extra-point kicker for five years, was not impaired by the fact that nearly all the toes of his right foot were severed in an elevator accident when he was eight years old. The present Giant kicking specialist, Pat Summerall, was born with a club foot. The doctor who operated on him soon after birth told Pat's mother that he would be able to lead a comparatively normal life but, of course, would not be able to run and play with the other boys.

Bobby Clatterbuck, who played quarterback for us several years ago, was cursed with poor eyesight. Off the field Bobby wore horn-rimmed glasses. During practice and on the infrequent occasions when he got into an actual game, he wore contact lenses. Since the quarterbacking duties were divided between Charlie and Arnold Galiffa at the time, Bobby warmed the bench. Weeks stretched into months. Then Cleveland came to town. Galiffa had been put out of action in the previous game, so Charlie was set to go all the way. On the first play from scrimmage a charging Brown lineman slammed Charles to the ground and he was carted from the field on a stretcher.

"Clatterbuck! Where's Clatterbuck?" the coach screamed on the sidelines.

"Here, Coach," came the nervous reply.

"Get in there!"

So Bobby fastened his chin strap and darted onto the field. The weeks of inactivity had not dulled his interest. He had been studying his play book with the assiduity of the most luminous star. His mind was ready for the big moment. His body was in top physical shape. But he had neglected one important detail: his contact lenses. Torn by the subconscious doubt that he would ever get into a game, Bobby had carelessly left the lenses in a tiny box on the shelf of his locker.

Haunted by the fuzzy images that catapulted at him from the void, he ticked off the plays from memory. The punishment he took was capital.

Finally, halftime came and Bob donned his contacts. The fact that he could now see his nemeses plainly did not prevent them from continuting to break through and inundate him on almost every play. To tell the truth, I think he was a bit happier with limited vision.

Deafness would not seem to be a particularly severe handicap for a football player. However, Giant halfback Alex Webster finds his affliction extremely annoying. After a mastoid operation, Alex was left completely deaf in one ear. In the huddle he simply turns his good ear toward the quarterback. No problem there. His troubles begin at the line of scrimmage. If the play calls for him to be stationed in his regular halfback position near the quarterback, he has no difficulty hearing the snap signal. If he is set out as a flanker, he looks down the line and moves forward as the ball is snapped. The revised man-in-motion series which the Giants favored several years ago presented Alex with his greatest problem. Even that one was overcome by a little cooperation. In this series Alex had to run laterally from the end position toward the quarterback and start forward at exactly the right instant. Since from that distance Alex could not hear the "Hut 1—Hut 2—Hut 3" count, the quarterback nodded his head as he began the signal, and Alex started counting to himself.

As he passed behind the quarterback, he had the opportunity to make certain they were synchronized.

One might think that the two positions above all others requiring peripheral vision would be quarterback and defensive halfback. Oddly, there have been men outstanding in both of these crucial spots who could see out of but one eye. This disability was apparently no handicap to Tommy Thompson, who quarterbacked the Eagles for eight years. Nor to Bobby Dillon, Green Bay safety man, who was designated "All Pro" many times during his career. Nor to former Colt halfback Bert Rechichar, who also holds the league record for the longest field goal—fifty-six yards.

Dillon and Rechichar played on the College All-Star squad the same year as Frank Gifford, who commented: "Among the three deep safety men on our team that day, there were only four eyes—two of them mine."

So don't despair if Junior isn't a perfect specimen. If he has talent, intelligence, determination, and self-control, he just might make the big leagues.

{17}

WHAT COST GLORY?

The hazards confronting a professional football player are many. Aside from the more obvious discomforts of damage to his physical well-being, there occurs another threat not so well known—that of damage to his reputation. Misguided souls sometimes misuse his name to further their own ends.

A professional football player (like the professional writer) is more vulnerable to imitators perhaps than others in the limelight. There's one reason: Although his name is well known, his face is usually unfamiliar to the general populace. A larcenous individual endowed with the proper physical proportions and a superficial knowledge of his chosen sport can alter his identity with little risk of immediate exposure.

Several years ago Lou Groza, long-time Cleveland Brown tackle and kicking specialist, bore the brunt of such dubious flattery. A man had for years passed himself off as Groza, from Florida to Pennsylvania. When the FBI finally tracked him down, he was laden with autographed pictures of himself in a football uniform bearing Lou's famous number 76. He had even appeared as Groza on a charity telethon in Jacksonville! Such philanthropic ventures were overshadowed by others more materialistic. Wealthy businessmen in several nearby states found they had made a slight error in lending the "gridiron star" money until "his mail caught up with him."

By coincidence, Charlie and I arrived in Savannah to visit friends a few days before the fake Groza was apprehended. We were greeted at the airport with the news that "our friend Lou" was in town and would join us for dinner. As soon as we got into the car, our host admitted frankly, "I should tell you before we go any farther that I don't care for your Mr. Groza. Brag, brag, brag, that's all he does. Daddy and I met him on the train, and we hadn't gone five miles before he whipped out a pile of press clippings and read to us about how great he is. And to tell the truth, I don't think he is particularly fond of you, Charles. When I told him you were coming to town, he got very nervous and started if-ing about a dinner engagement we've had for a week."

After several abortive attempts to refute the unflattering picture our friend had painted, Charlie shrugged and politely tried to change the subject. But his wife would not let it drop. Now I had never met Lou personally, but such unseemly conduct was certainly in contrast to the reputation of this gentleman and, in fact, untypical of pro football players in general. I opined loudly that we were dealing with an impostor. My persistence in continuing to analyze the clues which supported my claim caused

Charlie to dub me "Super Sleuth." We dined Groza-less that night as I had predicted, and the subsequent exposé presented me with an infrequent pleasure—the opportunity of saying "I told you so."

A car salesman's wife and son stopped by the office to join him for lunch one day. "Come here, Sonny, I've got something I bet you'd like to see," he beamed. "Frank Gifford's autograph—on a check. He just bought the biggest model we had in stock and will pick it up later this afternoon!"

His son was not impressed. "That's not Frank Gifford's autograph. He signed my program when Uncle John took me to the game last week. And he don't write like *that*."

This positive statement caused the salesman to recall certain unsettling features of the prior conversation. "You know, he did hem and haw when I asked him how Triplett was getting along. Didn't seem to know at first who I was talking about, much less the nature of Mel's injury."

Later, as the phony Gifford reached for the showroom door handle, the sight of the entire staff lined up in militant expectation evidently frightened him off. The con man bolted down the street and melted into the crowd.

Generally, however, these warped characters rate financial gain second to the thrill of "being somebody." Several years ago a benevolent stranger called from Los Angeles to report that a man was masquerading as Charlie Conerly in that city. As nearly as we could determine, the ersatz Conerly was not attempting to cash in heavily on his pose, but seemed content to mooch an occasional meal or drink and elaborate loudly on his prowess as a quarterback. Distance and Charlie's preoccupation with the title race made immediate action impractical. So we sat back to await further developments. Fortunately, there were none that we ever heard of.

A former Redskin once appeared as an "item" in a nationally syndicated column, after supposedly squiring a luscious model about town. His wife knew he was nowhere near the alleged scene of action. The newspaper later printed a retraction. But of course there were people who never learned the truth.

Several years ago we invited a vacationing Clarksdale couple to stop by following the Giant game they were to attend that afternoon. "I'm so anxious to see Eddie Price again," the wife exclaimed. "You know, we ran into him in Chicago last summer and took him out to dinner. He was up from New Orleans on business. Such a nice boy. A little conceited. But nice."

When Eddie, a Giant fullback, arrived, I steered him toward our friends, warning him from the side of my mouth that he had met them previously. Three blank looks ensued. Finally the wife shook her head. "That's not Eddie Price. Eddie Price is *this* tall." It took some doing, but we finally convinced the home folks that our Eddie was the genuine article.

"But Charlie," she insisted feebly. "That other Eddie knew so much about you . . . and the Giants . . . and even Tulane."

"And to think!" the husband moaned, "he ordered the most expensive steak on the Palmer House menu—and *I* picked up the check."

Possibly the prime roll of imitators during the past decade has been Johnny Lujack, ex-Notre Dame and Chicago Bear star. There were once three "Lujacks" operating in three different Eastern cities simultaneously!

More subtle means of using the good name of athletes to illegal advantage occasionally crop up. One of Kyle Rote's many talents is after-dinner speaking. Like many other qualified athletes past and present (Red Grange, Harry Mehre, the late Herman Hickman), Kyle makes a sideline business of filling banquet and club dates. December through March, until interest subsides in favor of baseball, Kyle averages three or four speaking engagements a week, mostly in the New York area, where he and his family now live.

Recently he was approached by an acquaintance who expressed regret that, after having been advertised as the main speaker at a certain club, Kyle had been unable to attend and had sent a last-minute substitute. Not quite aware of the implication, Kyle mumbled something about a mistake, thinking the man had confused him with someone else. Several days later, the identical situation arose, only another club was involved. Finally the light dawned. To stimulate interest and boost attendance at these meetings, the entertainment committees had boldly and dishonestly announced that Kyle had been engaged as speaker for the evening. Only after the meetings were called to order would the chairman arise and announce that due to circumstances of one kind or another, Mr. Rote had been unable to attend, and in his place . . .

The handsome ex-SMU standout determined to put a stop to such shenanigans. He knew the word would eventually get around that he was apparently treating his obligations lightly. He would be branded as irresponsible and unreliable. Legitimate offers were certain to become less frequent.

Quite by accident, Kyle discovered the third attempt to trade fraudulently on his reputation. While making a purchase at a local bookstore, he fell into casual conversation with another customer who was "looking forward" to hearing Kyle speak at a certain banquet a week hence. Taking note of the details, Kyle sped to his home and called his lawyer, whose advice was simple: "Contact the organization, tell them firmly you are aware of the situation, and demand twice your usual fee. For your future's sake, you must teach such people a lesson."

After the expected stammering and buck-passing and protestations of a mixup, the president finally agreed. Kyle said afterward, "I was so mad that night I guess my adrenal glands were super-stimulated. It was the best speech I ever made."

{18}

DODGERS AND DEVISERS

There are tricks in all trades, as we have just seen, and the game of football is no exception. Deceptions detrimental to the sport are sometimes devised, but are quickly eliminated by special rulings. Others, including some which have captured the imagination of the sports public, have been incorporated as standard procedure.

Before the turn of the century, Harvard's famous flying wedge was the scourge of hapless opponents. The chain of charging linemen holding tightly to each other formed an impenetrable phalanx, behind which the ballcarrier was able to make substantial gains unharassed. Other teams soon adopted the V-shaped blockbuster. The resulting brutality caused its elimination from the game. To forestall its reappearance the professional rule book forbids interlocking interference, defined as *the grasping of one and another by, or encircling body to any degree with, hands or arms by offensive players.*

The forward pass, in its early stages, confounded defenders and soon drew howls of protest from purists who claimed it was taking the foot out of football. Its increasing popularity, however, resulted in the gradual lifting of restrictions. The penalty for an incompletion was reduced in turn from loss of the ball to the opponents, to loss of fifteen yards, to loss of a down. It was not until much later, however, that forward passing graduated from limited use as a desperation maneuver to the integral part of the game as we know it today.

The rule which states that *no player shall wear any headgear or any equipment which* [the] *referee considers will confuse opponents due to their similarity to the ball* is designed to deter an old-time ruse of "Button, button, who's got the button?" As play began, all four backfield men would remove their helmets, making it difficult for opponents to distinguish the ballcarrier from the three helmet-carriers.

Wearing tennis or basketball shoes to improve footing on an ice-covered turf is now elemental. But in 1934 it was a revolutionary coup which enabled Steve Owen's Giants to slaughter the conventionally cleat-clad Bears on a frozen field in the championship game that year.

The tackle-eligible play was long permissible, but little used in National League competition. The Giants' successful use of Arnie Weinmeister as the tackle in question was probably responsible for its abolishment in 1951. Though his weight hovered near the 260 mark, Arnie was fleet of foot, having in fact seen some service at the fullback spot in college. In one variation, Arnie would line up at the line of scrimmage in his regular tackle position, but at the shift would change places with the end on his left.

Since eligible receivers at that time were designated as backfield men and "players on either end of the line," Arnie was then legally acceptable as a pass receiver. The elements of surprise and brute strength combined to make this "eligible tackle" a sometimes devastating weapon.

Incidentally, Arnie devised a crafty little scheme which concerned off-the-field teamwork—but only in the sense that he allowed his own private team to do all the work. The training season, with its far-flung exhibition games, requires that the squad take to the road quite frequently. During Arnie's tenure as a player the Giants traveled exclusively by train. Baggage was a bother. Each man was responsible for hauling his personal belongings about from train to hotel to stadium to train, etc. For Arnie the problem was somewhat magnified. A dapper man, his summer wardrobe required two large suitcases and an unwieldy suit bag. The resourceful Mr. Weinmeister hit on a clever method for eliminating the bother.

Prior to each scheduled trip he would approach an impressionable rookie with the following proposition: "Look, fellow. There's no need in both of us being encumbered with luggage on this trip. Tell you what—here's my compartment number. You leave my bag there and pick it up when we get to Chicago in the morning. And I'll take care of yours the next time we hit the road." Arnie's knack of speaking pleasantly but with a definite air of authority—coupled with the fact that first-year men generally stand in awe of such veteran performers—invariably resulted in success for the opening gambit of Arnie's three-part plan.

The second part dealt with a second rookie and the second suitcase, the third with a third rookie and the suit bag.

Somehow Arnie's turn to play porter never rolled around. And by the time he ran out of unsuspecting rookies, the regular season was underway, the bulk of his wardrobe was ensconced at his New York hotel, and only a small weekend case was needed for the out-of-town games. That, Arnie could manage by himself.

Cleveland coach Paul Brown is as noted for his messenger guards as he is for winning. The revolving linemen trot between bench and huddle before every offensive play to transmit Paul's instructions to his quarterback. Back in 1956 the Brown mentor decided to carry his personalized play-calling a bit further. He installed a transistor receiver in the helmet of the quarterback and began to broadcast person-to-person from the bench, thus eliminating the middleman.

This ingenious system of communication was highly successful for several weeks. Then the Browns met their traditional rivals, the Giants, and the bubble burst. It was almost as if the Giant defenders knew in advance what play the Clevelanders would run. And indeed they did. For, no laggards they, the New Yorkers had outfitted their bench with a transistor receiver tuned to Mr. B.'s frequency. A Giant player who had formerly served time with the Browns decoded the Cleveland signals and flashed the upcoming plays to his current defensive teammates, thereby endowing them with an uncanny clairvoyance.

Screams of robotism subsequently forced the abandonment of this electronic tea party.

An extremely colorful trick of the trade disappeared from the scene as the result of a rule change instituted several years ago.

This revision states: *During the last two minutes of either half, if the score is tied or the team in possession is behind in score and has exhausted* [the three] *legal time outs, an additional time out may be granted to remove an injured player from the field. However, the ball shall not be put into play for at least 10 seconds thereafter.*

In days gone by, the complexion of many games was changed by the agonized writhings of a gridiron actor whose timely "injury" stopped the clock, thereby providing his team with a few precious extra seconds in which to operate. Since the penalty for excessive time outs now involves loss of *time* rather than loss of yardage (sometimes both), such histrionics are futile.

No innovation in the history of the game has wielded such a salient effect on the injury rate. How marvelous that the addition of a simple paragraph to the NFL manual could be responsible for almost completely eliminating the distressing number of injuries which formerly occurred in the waning moments of a half!

It was a good show. I rather miss it.

As mentioned earlier, before each game the offensive and defensive coaches post the names of the players they have designated as regulars—those who will play in the game that day until otherwise notified. These men automatically run onto the field whenever the offensive and defensive units trade places.

A perennial Giant substitute became dissatisfied with his role as a "second-class citizen" several years ago and employed a combination of unauthorized ingenuity and fast footwork to rectify the frustrating situation. Whenever he felt like it, he would simply put *himself* into the game! Poised on the edge of the bench, his helmet already in place, he would streak for the field at the exchange, leaving his first-string counter-part standing open-mouthed on the sidelines, still fumbling with his chin strap.

This ruse was successful for quite a while because both the coach and the regular thought the other had requested the substitution. Even after the victim finally caught on, he was loathe to tell on his teammate and solved the problem himself by running a series of impromptu foot races with his would-be pre-emptor. In case of a tie he would give the twelfth man in the huddle a pseudo-quizzical look which sent him back to the bench feeling a mite foolish.

Another trick-of-the-trade attempt which backfired occurred in the Giant training camp. The original roster included a three-hundred-pound rookie lineman who, almost everybody agreed, had three speeds: start, stumble, and fall. However, he *was* big, and the coaches gave him every opportunity to make the team. Because of such formidable size, his presence on the practice field could hardly be overlooked. One day he was conspicuous by his absence.

"Where is old Three Speed?" head coach Jim Lee Howell thundered. There was a long, tense silence. "I think he's back at the dormitory," a player volunteered.

Jim stormed into the building. Skipping practice is an unpardonable sin. And there was the absentee stretched out on his bed half-asleep. Jim sputtered.

The huge rookie leaped to attention. "Well, coach," he explained patiently, "I decided that for the good of the team I'd leave off the morning practice. By working out just once a day I could save up my energy and be that much more valuable in the afternoon."

Jim's vocabulary does not include profanity, but his two-word reply, "Get packed!" blighted the grass on the practice field three hundred yards away.

Other dodges and devices are harmless or helpful. Doak Walker, speedy Detroit Lion halfback, also earned his keep by kicking extra points and field goals. Since calling time out before each kick to change from his running slipper into the bulkier kicking shoe would have been impractical, the ex-SMU ace devised a way to complete the operation well within the thirty-second time limit between plays. He had the time-honored shoe lace replaced with a zipper.

The adhesive tape binding with which Negro tackle Roosevelt Brown strengthens his weak wrists stands out like a beacon. To prevent officials from calling every sudden move he makes "illegal use of the hands," Rosie carefully gives the bandages a coat of shoe polish before each game.

A master stroke in the use of the power of suggestion as a tactical maneuver occurred in a league game one year.

A fracas involving two opposing linemen drew the disapproval of the officials. One burly tackle was ejected from the game; but in the confusion, the referee lost sight of the other fighter. At that moment a teammate of the missing player, noting the moment of indecision exclaimed quickly, as if in anger—"You can't throw 78 out of the game. He didn't start it." The official wheeled and shouted to the innocent-looking No. 78, sitting on the end of the bench: "You are barred from further competition in today's game!"

No wonder the poor fellow was so wide-eyed. Because of injury, 78 hadn't played in a game in three weeks!

19

DOING SOMETHING ABOUT THE WEATHER

The rain check, an accepted feature of baseball, is foreign to pro football. Neither snow, nor rain, nor heat, nor gloom of night stays these athletes from the dogged completion of their regularly scheduled games. The football season is squeezed in between the heat of the baseball season and the extremes of winter weather. At that, there is an overlap on both ends. Simply not enough time is available for allotting alternate days in the event of inclement weather. The players play.

This unyielding adherence to the agenda sometimes works a hardship on the most stalwart of fans, but think of the umbrella-less, raccoon coat-less, brandy-less players on the field! Several Giant games stand out as impressive examples of havoc caused by weather.

The Giant-Washington game played in Griffith Stadium in 1960 was almost canceled—not because of the snow which blanketed the field to a depth of four inches (games occasionally take place under similar conditions)—but because the deluge rested atop the protective tarpaulin. Whenever the weatherman predicts rain or snow for the weekend, the playing field is covered with five twenty-yard strips of heavy canvas in an attempt to preserve decent footing for the players. This giant "raincoat" (which costs about ten thousand dollars) is removed just prior to game time. "Light snow flurries" had been forecast for that Sunday morning. The Redskin management was shocked by the weatherman's masterful under statement.

The game was delayed about forty minutes while the regular ground crew, augmented by a makeshift, hurriedly recruited squad of seventy-five helpers, made a vain attempt to remove the tarpaulin from the field. The seventy-five were for the most part misdemeanants bailed out for the occasion from the local jail. The prevailing weakness must have involved intoxication; most retained a slight glow. Every few minutes as they first struggled with the huge canvas, a cry of "Man under!" would ring out, and operations had to be suspended while the unfortunate was dragged from beneath the tarp. They finally got a twenty-yard strip halfway off before realizing the futility of the project. And there it lay, piled up in the middle of the field.

Two trucks, one pulling, the other pushing, finally succeeded in shoving the huge roll to the sidelines.

During the disorder, Giant owner Jack Mara encountered Redskin owner George Preston Marshall bustling along the sidelines, a smile of eminent satisfaction lighting his face. "Well, Jack, they're on the way!" Marshall sang out.

"The snowplows?" inquired Mara hopefully.

The tone of the inveterate showman's reply was almost condescending: "No—the snow boots for our band!"

Meanwhile, back in the dressing room—runners periodically popped in to report on the lack of progress afield, and the players were assailed with conflicting opinions as to whether or not the game could take place. The final decision set a precedent: Never before had an NFL game been played on top of a tarpaulin.

Since there were no yard lines to guide them, officials had to estimate first downs. In the early stages of the game, Charlie questioned a decision of the referee. "He told me that for once his rulings might be slightly inaccurate, but he would do the best he could under the circumstances and we'd just have to take his word. I really felt foolish because I realized that he was right, of course, and I didn't complain again."

Later, Pat Summerall slogged onto the field to attempt a point after touchdown kick. "Usually," Pat told us that night, "Charlie [the holder] has some encouraging comment or settling advice to offer, like: 'Nice and easy, Pat. Keep your head down.' But today when I trotted up, he was shaking his head in disbelief and mumbling, 'What in the world am I doing here? A man thirty-nine years old—out *playing in the snow!*' After that remark I was still snickering so hard I almost missed the point."

The Giants triumphed in the fiasco, 17–3, and they never once touched the ground.

The muddiest affair I can remember took place in 1955 when the Cardinals met the Giants at the Polo Grounds. Despite the fact that the turf had been covered all week, the field was a sodden mess. After the first two plays, the players were so completely smeared with mud that every number was obliterated. The announcer was in a state of utter confusion in his attempt to credit the proper men with runs and tackles—as were we all.

Punts and kick-offs were laughable. The ball would make a resounding splash as it struck the quagmire and often remained embedded on end. There was one particularly low spot in the infield in which water was standing shoetop high. If an official was a mite slow in retrieving the ball at the end of a play, it sometimes floated away! It was in this area that Kyle Rote caught one of the few passes thrown that day and splashed down the field for a substantial gain. Upon being tackled, he fell face down and skidded ten yards with his nose in the goo before coming to a halt. Being tackled was easier than the slide. "I almost drowned," recalls Kyle, "before I could get untangled and wipe enough mud from my face to get a deep breath. I really was scared."

A Cardinal player had an even closer call. It was his misfortune to be on the bottom of a heavy pile-up involving six or eight men. By the time the slimy group could unfold and free him, the poor fellow was unconscious. He was quickly transported to the sidelines, where artificial respiration was applied to revive him.

Several years ago the wind played a dirty trick on the kick-off specialist of the Baltimore Colts. Having placed the ball down on his own forty as required, Steve Myhra redoubled his efforts for a kick into the twenty-five mile-per-hour wind and sent the pigskin up-up-up. A capricious gust caught the ball, which sailed back over the astonished kicker's head and landed on the twenty-three-yard line—a loss of seventeen yards!

The hottest day for football in my memory dawned in Memphis, Tennessee, where the Giants engaged the Bears in an exhibition game in August of 1951. The thermometer hovered near the ninety-seven-degree mark in the stands and probably registered fifteen degrees warmer on the playing field, which was completely enclosed and therefore devoid of the slightest hint of breeze. The humidity was suffocatingly high; and the fact that the team had previously been stationed for training in the cool clime of upstate New York provided a shocking contrast. After the first series of downs the players were wringing wet. After several, many found it difficult to breathe and staggered to the sidelines, summoning replacements. Spectators were falling out like flies, and players were treated for heat exhaustion en masse. The defense worked like fiends attempting to turn the ball over to the offense, thereby gaining a respite on the bench. Charlie, a wiry specimen, lost only seven pounds during the encounter; some of his meatier teammates shed as many as eighteen.

Later the same year the Giants played a game which rivaled the antics of the Keystone Cops for low comedy. The scene: Yankee Stadium. The rivals: The Giants and the defunct New York Football Yankees. The time: mid-December. The temperature: fifteen degrees. A week of rain had preceded the contest, during which time the field was dutifully covered with a protective tarpaulin. However, since a hard freeze was predicted for Saturday night, the groundskeepers were directed to take away the canvas for fear it would freeze to the turf, making removal impossible the next day.

Both events occurred on schedule. The tarp was taken off. The freeze set in. As a result, the field was covered with a sheet of ice half an inch thick in spots.

Players on both teams wore the conventional basketball shoes designed to aid footing. Ice skates would have been more practical. Standing itself was a feat of no mean accomplishment; running, practically impossible. The stands howled as player after player took spectacular pratfalls.

Somehow the Giants attained a substantial lead, but finally the Yanks got a break. After catching a short pass, their star end headed for the goal line fifty yards away—in a dead walk. As each Giant tackler lunged toward him, he simply stood still for a moment and calmly watched his adversary slide helplessly by. At last he was all alone—within fifteen yards of pay-dirt (or pay-ice, if you prefer).

The excitement of near-success evidently affected his balance and suddenly his feet flew out from under him. By this time the defenders far downfield had risen and were carefully walking toward him. Had the "runner" continued his strategy of slow, deliberate movement, he might have made it. Instead, his aplomb gone, he thrashed about furiously in a desperate effort to stand up. Closer and closer skated the defenders in slow motion. Harder and harder the ballcarrier struggled. I could almost hear the piano playing tied-to-the-railroad-track music in the background. The villains finally reached the frustrated fellow and sat on him carefully, ending his bid for a touchdown.

The universal desire for a happy ending caused even Giant fans to set up a resounding cheer when the Yankees scored several plays later.

20

BOOS

Stormy weather? . . . No reminiscence would be complete without some mention of The Lean Years—when the Polo Grounds was festooned with *Back to the farm, Conerly* signs; when catcalls rang out because Charlie often found it necessary to "eat the ball"; and when newspaper accounts of Giant games were frequently unfriendly.

I am told that human nature kindly endows us with the tendency to suppress unpleasant memories and recall more vividly the happier experiences. Nevertheless, in answer to a question about how the foregoing unpleasantries affected our lives, I could not, in good conscience, admit to anything so dramatic as a poignant family scene, fraught with emotion, in which either Charlie or I was visibly desolated by the press notices or the signs or the boos. Not even for the sake of a good story.

I am sure the expressions of disapproval left their scars, but Charlie is a master at hiding his feelings . . . even from me. Describing him as a stoic would not be far from the truth. He never complains. He never offers an alibi. He rarely allows disappointment to affect him. (Exceptions: an unsatisfactory game of cards or golf.) He accepts undeserved criticism and valid censure with equal calm—and without expressing malice toward his detractors in either case. The ravings of his severest critics after a poor performance could never compare with the reproach he gave himself.

As for me, I am a most un-stoical creature. I *do* complain. I alibi. I can always manage to find someone or something to share the blame for anything. Therefore, I too am able to exhibit a calm exterior in the face of adversity. I live in a little world where I am Queen, and the unseemly subjects who berate My King are several kinds of idiot. I must admit that I was taken aback when exposed for the first time to a thunderous chorus of boos directed at Charlie. I had been reared in accordance with my parents' practice that "If you can't say something nice about somebody, don't say anything at all." And of course in college, fans blame the *coach* for everything. I really believe the worst part of it all is feeling the eyes of the other wives as they look sympathetically down the row to see my reaction to the uncomplimentary vocalizing. But I just used to sit there, staring straight ahead, playing Queen.

I think it actually became fashionable to boo Charlie in the early fifties. In one game he completed the first nine passes he threw. When the tenth fell incomplete, the stands booed lustily!

Miles of copy have been written about the fact that the protection given Charlie by his line some years left something to be desired—and that his receivers in those days were not always terribly sure-fingered. I have had players apologize to *me* after a game in which Charlie absorbed a particularly stout drubbing.

"I'm just not big enough," an offensive guard told me once. "I weigh 220 and some of those guys across from me weigh 260. I just can't keep them off of Charlie. What makes it worse, he never complains. Just once I wish he'd give me a little hell in the huddle. It wouldn't make me try any harder, cause I'm trying as hard as I can right now, but I think I'd feel better."

Occasionally shouts of abuse are directed at the wives, but I never reply in kind because that would gratify the insulters. Boo birds are practiced in their art. They have a repertoire of standard replies with which I could never compete and are anxious for the opportunity to play comedian for their fellows. Generally when people sitting near us realize we are players' wives, they tactfully tone down any uncomplimentary remarks that come to mind.

However, after one game during which the Stadium air had been rent with cries of "Get Conerly outa there. We want Heinrich!" a very excited woman was waiting for us at the end of the wives' row. As we approached, she began to shake her fist and shout, "Your husbands stank today, the bums! Especially that bum Conerly!" And on and on.

I ignored her tirade, pretending I was somewhere else (waltzing in the palace ballroom, perhaps). But the fair complexion of the wife walking with me always belies her fiery temper. Whenever she becomes unduly excited a spot of brilliant red appears on each cheek. (We often tease her with, "What's the matter now, Barbara? You've got your clown rouge on.")

Barbara sprang into action. "Let me tell you one thing . . ." she began, her nose almost touching that of the vehement dissident.

The woman was startled, but not silenced. "Eat the ball! Eat the ball! That's all that dumb coward Conerly knows how to do . . ."

Barbara's cheeks turned the color of strawberry soda. "It's obvious that you don't know anything about football or you'd know it takes guts to eat the ball and be plowed under two or three big linemen. Dumb, you say? I'll have you know it takes quick thinking and skill to deliberately throw the ball away when your receivers are covered— just close enough to your own man so the official can't call it intentional grounding, but far enough from the defender covering him to prevent an interception. And if Charlie had had a line in front of him today, he wouldn't have had to do either . . ."

"You must be Mrs. Conerly," the woman jeered.

"No. I am Mrs. *Heinrich!*" Barb replied grandly. Whirling, she took me by the arm and flounced up the steps as only Barbara Heinrich can flounce.

Meanwhile, down on the field . . . "I guess all pro players have 'rabbit ears,'" Charlie observes, "but I imagine quarterbacks have the most sensitive hearing of all. At the Polo Grounds, in order to reach the playing field, we had to pass within a few feet of a section of bleacherites who evidently spent most of their spare time between Sundays thinking up new insults. I think it was a kind of game with them to see who could come up with the cleverest abuse. The fastest running I did on any Sunday was sprinting past that section. I'd always put on my helmet too—to help drown out the static. I don't think the remarks affected my performance one way or the other. But it gets to some fellows. Maybe we should have put up some of those signs they have in zoos: 'Please don't annoy the animals'!" Sometimes they would actually lean down and take a swipe at us as we ran by. I'm glad no one ever succeeded in hitting me. I couldn't have ignored that."

As a matter of fact, Charlie did slap a "fan" once. I got the word first from one of the players who preceded him to the apartment after the game. "Well, Charlie hit a kid today," he said, smiling. "I was standing right there and I don't blame him a bit."

I was frantic. A series of imaginary headlines flashed through my mind. POOR SPORT CONERLY ATTACKS CHILD. FATHER INSTITUTES MILLION DOLLAR SUIT. My fears were calmed somewhat as the story unfolded. On the way to the dressing room after a Giant loss, Charlie had been accosted by an unruly teenager, who was as tall as he and much stockier. The big youth cursed Charlie, who ignored him and tried to pass. He blocked his path and began to shove Charlie, calling him every vile name he could think of.

"Take your hands off me . . ." Charlie began. His warning was interrupted as the teenager drew back and threw a punch which glanced off Charlie's shoulder. Charlie slapped him in the face, hard, and ambled off the field.

"I guess I should have turned the other shoulder," he told me later. "I can take the talk, but when somebody starts shoving me around . . ."

Ironically, though the incident followed a Giant defeat, newspaper accounts described the game as "one of Charlie's finest performances." Perhaps the frustrated youngster had bet his week's allowance—from the Parole Board—on the Giants. Or his hard-earned wages—after selling hubcaps.

With the exception of an occasional "Ya bum ya!" directed at Charlie by a dissatisfied customer who recognized him on the street, such expressions of discontent were generally confined to game day. However, one extracurricular demonstration stands out in my memory. Back in 1952 or 1953 the Giants and their wives were invited by the management of Madison Square Garden to attend a Ranger game. Since many of us had never seen ice hockey played, over half the team accepted. We were enjoying the thrilling sport immensely, but our pleasure was short-lived. During an intermission (or third-time) the announcer boomed: "As the guests of the Garden, sitting in section so-and-so, we have the members of the New York Football Giants and their wives. Please stand."

As we rose, the rafters rang with the most deafening booing I have ever heard. I was taken so by surprise that the smile froze on my face, and not until Charlie tugged on my arm did I realize that I was the only one of our group still standing. We decided that only poor sports would leave before the game was over. Besides, we were afraid of another unpleasant demonstration should we stand up again, now that our position had been exposed. So we sat uncomfortably throughout the game, the object of insulting clichés shouted by wiseacres from a safe distance whenever there was a lull in the proceedings.

We lingered until the Garden was nearly empty in order to make our exit as inconspicuous as possible. As we began to shuffle out, a lone dissident far above us on the top row began to bombard Charlie with unflattering epithets. We ignored him. The affronts continued. What the little fellow lacked in stature, he made up in volume.

"Let me handle this, Charlie," offered Arnie Weinmeister, a soft-spoken, but fearsome tackle of gigantic proportions. Arnie shouted, "Hey, up there!" at the same time taking three or four giant steps toward the vocalizer.

The jeer-leader did not wait to see that Arnie had no intention of real pursuit, but turned and scurried out the nearest exit with an astounding burst of speed.

"We ought to catch that fellow and sign him up as a halfback. He's faster than anybody on the team," cracked Bill Austin.

Jim Duncan smiled. "Yeah, but who could catch him?"

The sting of such incidents was mitigated by a constant trickle of encouraging letters from loyal fans.

Though the scrapbook contains at least one write-up describing every Giant game since 1948, the "bad" games are noticeably less well represented than the good. This inequity stems not from any attempt at whitewashing, but from a dearth of clippings which allude to the unhappier contests. On any ordinary day Charlie often buys and reads all seven New York daily papers; but after an unfortunate game, he resists the temptation.

"I don't mind being knocked when I deserve it, and there are plenty of times I do," he explains. "But *I* know when I play poorly, and reading some reporter's description of it isn't going to help me improve. I'd probably just get mad at some nice guy who is only doing his job. They have to write what they see—but I don't have to read it."

When one of these bad reviews fall into my hands, I am likely to mutter darkly: "One would think you were the only man on the field today . . ."

To which he replies philosophically, "And reading some of the flattering write-ups of games we won, you might think the same thing. The quarterback receives more than his rightful share of the credit when things go well, so he should be prepared to accept a lion's share of the blame when they don't."

After years of careful consideration (and practical experience) I have arrived at certain conclusions concerning the practice of booing at professional football games. Likely the custom has its roots in ancient Rome, where spectators attending various exhibitions of manly skill and courage commonly expressed disapproval of a gladiator's unsatisfactory performance by turning "thumbs down." Happily, today's losers live to play another day. Therefore, since booing neither influences a coach's decision nor spurs a player to greater effectiveness, it serves no practical purpose other than calling attention to the booer—which is probably the whole idea, after all.

Leaning heavily on an overactive imagination and a vague memory of a course in freshman psychology, I have relegated the booers to several categories. Boos come from:

1. The fellow in the company of friends who know little about football and consider him something of an expert. To prove that he does indeed have a full grasp of the subject he sprinkles his enlightened explanations of the proceedings with rousing catcalls emitted at the slightest provocation.
2. His friends.
3. The same fellow in the company of his girl friend.
4. His girl friend.
5. The extrovert who has come to the game alone and wishes to strike up a conversation with his neighbors.
6. His neighbors.
7. The introvert who is browbeaten all week by a domineering employer and, unable to strike back at his boss, transfers his wrath to the players on the field, thereby gaining an outlet for his pent-up emotions. (Psychiatrists might do well to recommend this type of therapy to patients suffering from insecurity and inferiority complexes.)
8. The man sitting on his left.
9. The introvert who is browbeaten by his wife.
10. The man sitting on his right.

11. A category already hinted at in numbers 2, 4, 6, 8, and 10 results in Dr. Conerly's maxim: People sitting next to people who boo, boo too. It seems to be a form of mass hysteria participated in by impressionable people caught up in the spirit of the occasion—a mild form of mob violence.

12. The fellow who has come to the game only to get away from the kids for a few hours. He really doesn't know what is happening and therefore is bored. An occasional good boo helps immeasurably to relieve the monotony.

13. The small man who tried out for the team in high school and was told by the coach, "Son, come back when you grow six inches and gain thirty pounds." He has had no trouble adding the pounds these last ten years, but unfortunately got no taller. He delights in venting his frustration on the king-sized players, all of whom represent the star tackle who stole his girl in high school.

14. The big fellow who was told by his high school coach, "Son, come back when you have lost thirty pounds." Folks still call him "Tubby."

How does Charlie feel about being the object of spectator disapproval? Mr. C. contends that the ticket purchased by the malcontent entitles him to express any opinion he might hold—however loudly.

How do I react? I locate the knavish songbird, place him in one of the foregoing categories, and mentally summon the Royal Executioner.

{21}

CHEERS

Mail is an interesting, often satisfying part of a professional football player's life. Usually, it is the reverse of booing. Most of the letters he receives are complimentary. Ninety percent consists of requests by small boys for autographs and/or pictures. Five percent comes from junior high school boys seeking tips concerning training and strategy. The rest is an assortment of communications, nearly all quaint, from adults.

Like most players, Charlie answers his fan mail personally. I occasionally help by separating the assembly-line communications that state merely, "I collect autographs. Please send me yours," from the letters and cards with a little more sincerity or interest.

Some years ago, so that he could fulfill requests for autographed pictures, I had a supply of post cards imprinted with his likeness. Sometimes I type the addresses on these, but Charlie reads each incoming letter and writes the reply himself. He has been known to fall behind in answering his mail but always manages to get the job done sooner or later. However, he is often stopped by lack of a return address or by those scrawled in childish illegibility.

Perhaps the most wistful letter came from a teenager in Minnesota. "I think you are the greatest quarterback in the world," it began. "And my life would be complete if you could teach me to play quarterback. I would like to come to Mississippi and spend the summer. I would sleep in the barn or anywhere and do any kind of hard work to earn my keep."

Charlie pondered for a week about how to answer that one. He finally explained to the boy that Charlie's parents, not we, live on the farm, and that our little house in town is too small to accommodate more than two people for any length of time. He suggested that the writer's high school coach was probably just as qualified to undertake instructions of this nature, quoted the old line, "Practice makes perfect," and signed off with the truism that such determination would surely lead to success in this and other ventures.

I have often wondered what happened to the subject of a letter written by a distraught father in 1958. "My eight-year-old son is so heartbroken because the Giants lost the championship game to the Colts that he has not eaten a bite in three days," he wrote. "Please write him a little note about being a good loser. His mother and I are at wit's end. . . ." Naturally, as soon as he received it, Charlie hastened to remedy the distressing situation with a letter of consolation. However, the time element involved conjured up visions of a very skinny eight-year-old. Charlie might have wired or called except that the frenzied letter was sent to Yankee Stadium and we had already left for home. The Stadium staff sent it along to the Giant office, which was closed for the holidays. Finally it reached our Clarksdale address—several days after we had gone off for a short post-season vacation. In all, three weeks elapsed before Charlie got his hands on the plaintive message!

The letters that appeal to me most are those from the littlest of the little fellows—carefully printed on lined paper, with an "E" here and there turned backwards.

> Dear Charlie Conerly,
> I love you, Charlie Conerly. I want to
> be just like you when I grow up.
> Love,
> Stevie

Such simple eloquence reminds us that, whether he likes it or not, the athlete (professional and otherwise) is a symbol of perfect manhood to youngsters everywhere. And the obligation to furnish a decent example cannot be ignored.

Judging from the handwriting, the following request was from a boy about twelve years old: "I am writing to you, Mr. Conerly, because I think you know this. I want to know what makes a good football player?"

In my opinion, Charlie's reply embodies the essence of the game of football, though I'm sure he was unaware that his statement would be later termed profound by an admiring wife with a sense of the dramatic. He answered: "Let's take a certain amount of talent and intelligence for granted. Outside of that, there are two attributes which sum up all the things a football player must do—and have—to be classed as a good football player: intense desire and a complete disregard for pain."

The latter qualification, incidentally, has ramifications which are sometimes unfortunate for the wife of a player. Charlie's reaction to the minor aches and ills of others is something less than Albert Schweitzer–like. Yowling through the house one night on my way from the kitchen to the medicine cabinet, I noted in some consternation that the husband (whom I passed en route) did not look up from his book. Having treated my wounds, I stopped by the couch, moaning audibly, to show him that my hand had been blistered (slightly) by a splatter of hot grease. He marked his place carefully, looked up, and said,

"Oh?"

The temptation to reward his comforting bedside manner with a left hook (my right hand was bandaged) was almost overpowering. However, the memory of scenes far more common in our family circle stayed my good hand.

My first question to Charlie after a game is always, "Did you get hurt?" Unless his leg is in a splint or his arm in a sling, the answer is always, "No." One Wednesday, having received the usual negative reply, I happened to walk into the bathroom while he was shaving. For the first time I noticed that his left shin was a mass of deep, angry slashes that would have put me on crutches for a week.

"I thought you told me you didn't get hurt last Sunday!"

He glanced down briefly. "Just cleat marks." And returned to his razor.

It is fairly natural for players who have such offhand concern for their own ailments to develop a certain intolerance for other people's minor complaints.

When injured, Charlie appreciates the influx of home remedies in the mail. Naturally, some are quite farfetched; some even tinged more than slightly with superstition. Occasionally the suggested treatments sound reasonable enough to prompt Charlie to ask Dr. Sweeny's opinion of them. The team physician replies, sadly, "Charlie, if you want to try that, we will. I doubt that it will help, but it might. And it certainly won't hurt anything."

Useful or not, the letters impart a sense of well-being in knowing that people are not only concerned about his health, but will take the time and trouble to try to help.

In a story about Charlie carried by a national magazine several years ago, he was quoted as saying: "I haven't decided what I'll do when my football career is over. In a game I get a feeling I'm sure I'll never find anywhere else."

Several days later he received a letter signed "Solar Student No. 815620," who said *he* knew where. The writer went on to describe the ecstasy resulting from drinking the juice of a certain cactus plant indigenous to Mexico, detailing the shivers of joy and the feeling of complete euphoria produced by only small amounts. He gave references for further study of the subject and tips about obtaining guides for the trek to the interior where the precious plant grows. We filed the letter away under "L," for Last Resort.

The same article was accompanied by a photograph of Charlie sitting dejectedly in the dressing room after a loss. Unintentionally, the camera caught a distant full-length view of Lindon Crow (ex-Southern Cal ace) clad only in a bewildered look. Lindon's mail took an interesting turn that week. Crow fan clubs sprang up around the country. One high schooler wrote: "All the girls in my gym class have that dreamy picture of you pasted on our lockers. The fellows can have their *Playboys*. We'll take more swinging photos like that one any day!"

Letters from star-struck girls are fairly common. Pat Summerall recalls a letter he received when he played for the Cardinals. It was from a girl who had gone to the University of Arkansas when he had. "But you probably wouldn't remember me." She'd like to see him some time; etc. Being married, Pat noted only the flattering good taste of the letter writer and dismissed it from his mind. Several weeks later, his locker mate called to his attention a charming communication he had received from an ex-school mate (female). "You probably won't remember me, but I was at Colorado the same time you were," it began.

"Hey!" shouted an eavesdropper down the line. "That's the girl who was at Florida the same time I was."

One of my favorite letters to Charlie bore a New England postmark. "The controversy about your true age has raged so violently among our office staff that we have set up a pool, with the closest estimate taking down the cash. I have been commissioned to write to you in order to settle this argument once and for all." I answered that one on his behalf, giving the correct data for the permanent peace of mind of those concerned. September 19, 1921.

On one occasion a fan found the mails inadequate and deemed it necessary to express his disapproval of a Giant defeat in person. Frank Gifford, incapacitated by a leg injury, lay helpless in his hospital bed early one morning, thinking perhaps about the double disappointment of the Sunday before. Suddenly in the half-light he made out the hulking form of a huge man, six-foot-six and weighing at least three hundred pounds, most of which had slipped from chest to stomach with the passing years.

"Hey, you Gifford!" he shouted into the silence. "What's wrong with you guys?" Too startled to speak, Frank stared openmouthed. The behemoth answered his own question: "I'll tell you what's wrong. It's that Jim Lee Howell." Grasping the foot of the bed, he rattled it fiercely, continuing an incoherent tirade against the Giant head coach.

"I'll admit I was scared to death," said Frank later. "It was so dark and he was so big. With the bum leg I knew I couldn't move if the idiot decided to attack me. I inched my hand over until I got a firm grip on the water pitcher sitting on the bedside table—just in case. Finally I found my voice. "How—how (it didn't sound like me at all) did you get in here?"

For the first time, the monster smiled. "I told the nuns on duty I was your brother."

"Well," said Frank, getting braver all the time, "Jim Lee is the one you want to talk to. He'll be at Yankee Stadium at ten o'clock."

With that, the awesome stranger turned on his heel and left. "I had no idea he would follow the thing through," said Frank. "I was just intent on getting him out of my room."

But the malcontent was as persevering as he was huge. A few minutes before ten the early arrivals among the Giant players were chatting leisurely in the meeting room at the Stadium waiting for the daily proceedings to begin. Suddenly the door burst open and Frank's friend strode in. "I'll show you guys how to throw a block!" he screamed as he lunged at a large desk, knocking it awry. As an attention-getting device, this was eminently successful. A stunned hush fell over the group, and the players looked in wide-eyed disbelief at the intruder.

"Hey, Modzelewski! What were you doing out there Sunday, playing tiddlywinks?" he shouted, directing the question to Harlan Svare. He continued to elaborate upon the performance of half a dozen players, whom he knew by name but evidently not by sight. "The real trouble with this team is the coach. Where's Howell? I'll show him how to run this team." He punctuated his remarks by snatching six or eight footballs from a box on the desk and drop-kicking them in quick succession across the room.

The police, called by an eavesdropping trainer, finally arrived and dragged the struggling mammoth away. His parting shot was classic: "All right, so you don't appreciate me. I'll go down to Baltimore and help Johnny Unitas out."

H-m-m, I wonder . . . perhaps he did.

{22}

A PRO'S PROPOSITIONS

"For you," I nodded, handing Charlie the phone, and bolted for the kitchen to rescue the chicken (smoldering Southern fried, of course). "It's somebody you don't know," I shouted over my shoulder. "He wants to speak to 'Chuck.'"

("Chuck" is strictly a newspaper appellation. His New York friends call him "Charlie." Mississippi friends call him "Roach." His mother calls him "Charles." When in New York I try to remember to call him "Charlie" instead of "Roach" in public so I'll be spared the chore of explaining that this earthy sobriquet has its shadowy roots in the lost mysteries of childhood. Neither of us knows where or why it originated.)

After extinguishing the chicken, I returned to eavesdrop. Charlie's conversation, a series of tentative "Yes, uh-huh's" with an occasional nervous laugh, was suddenly interrupted by a positive negative: "No—not *me!*"

Then: "No, I don't think anybody on the team would."

My curiosity was piqued.

"Some guy wanted me to dive off a sixty-foot tower," Charlie explained afterward. "I've had fans suggest I take a flying leap, but they've never been this explicit before." The unorthodox proposal was the brainchild of an over-enthusiastic advertising agent.

The incident brought to mind wild schemes proposed in all seriousness to others on the team. While Pat Summerall was with the Chicago Cardinals, he received a cryptic telegram: "If you want to make $10,000 in one month, call this number in Pennsylvania, collect . . ."

"Couldn't be a bribe offer," Pat mused. "The season's almost over." He mulled over the intriguing situation for a full thirty seconds and sprinted for the nearest phone. The proponent was a fifty-five-year-old furniture manu-facturer who did a bit of drop-kicking on the side. The gentleman had designed a goal post with a target attached in the center of the crossbar. It was his plan for the two kicking specialists to hold a barn-storming exhibition tour throughout the South.

He waxed ecstatic, then added a touch of realism: "How many spectators could you guarantee in Lake City, Florida (Pat's hometown)?"

"My wife might come," ventured Pat.

Undaunted by this obvious cynicism, the gentleman began to quote estimates concerning the amount of money required to initiate the project—and Pat would have to put up only half.

The pride of Lake City finally was able to terminate the conversation with the "Don't call me . . ." cliché.

Several years ago offensive captain Kyle Rote received a call from a man who had a splendid idea for fostering team spirit. It seems the man owned a pair of Great Danes who would be trained to gallop full tilt around the edge of the field after each Giant touchdown—for a slight rental fee. Kyle referred him to the Giant front office.

Lindon Crow, talented defensive halfback, was at one time on the public relations staff of a national cigarette company. One of his principal duties involved presenting before the various organizations in his territory a program which consisted generally of a film depicting the highlights of the previous seasons's NFL games, a short explanatory talk, and an informal question-and-answer period.

One spring Lindon was booked to appear before a captive audience—the inmates of San Quentin Prison. ("They smoke too.") The show met with the most enthusiastic response in Lindon's career. ("They love football.") Afterwards Lindon mingled with the prisoners, shaking hands and answering questions. Suddenly one little fellow pulled him aside and, glancing furtively around, detailed a plan for making both of them fabulously wealthy men. All Lindon would be required to do was promote a marvelous invention—a cover for book matches that was perfectly plain on the outside. The inventor's eyes glowed as he explained that only when the matches were *wet* did the advertisement become visible!

Even the Giant wives have been confronted with imaginative projects. Unfortunately, we once took the bait.

Several years ago an advertising agency approached a group of us with a proposition. Would we act as models for a line of toreador pants which resembled football britches? In lieu of a fee, we would be allowed to keep "the modish and very expensive pants." Sounded like fun, and we tentatively agreed.

A subsequent call added the stipulation that we bring our husbands, who would outfit themselves in uniform to be photographed standing behind us. That requirement let me out, for Charlie had a previous commitment— an opportune conflict, as it happened. Each girl was instructed to wear bobby socks, loafers, and a loose white sweater, on which would be pinned a number corresponding to that of her husband.

Things took a turn for the worse almost immediately upon their arrival at Yankee Stadium, the scene of action. First of all, the pants were elasticized and indecently snug. Then the photographer developed a sudden interest in the back of the pants and insisted that the girls pose bending over in imitation of a huddle, while he sighted from the rear. They rebelled, and he grudgingly took a few front-view shots. These were merely window dressing after all, for it evolved that the star of the show was a sultry professional model (with an eighteen-inch waist) who suddenly materialized on the field. She was clad not in bobby socks, loafers, and a "sloppy joe," but in fancy high heels and a skin-tight sweater. The girls also admitted that she looked somewhat better than they in the notorious toreadors.

The photographer took scores of shots of the model cavorting with the boys while the wives fidgeted on the sidelines. They realized too late that the whole idea was a clever ruse designed to circumvent the fee usually paid to pro footballers for such work.

Well, as we say in the trade: "You can't win 'em all." To this comforting philosophy, the wives added a line or two, more original but less printable.

{23}

THE GAMES OF MEMORY

It would be impractical to document—or even to mention—all of the memorable games in a career as long as Charlie's. He has played in well over 150 contests since he joined the Giants in 1948. However, by recalling a few which for various reasons stand out in his mind or mine, perhaps I can reveal to some extent the impact of professional football on our lives. Some memories are sweet. Some are bitter. Some are . . . well—

Charlie's very first professional game made a lasting impression—on his face. In this initial encounter he received an injury diagnosed by Dr. Sweeny as "a severe cheekbone depression." Even today, some fourteen years later, close examination will reveal a slight indentation in the right side of his face.

Charlie's pro baptism occurred in the 1948 league opener against the defunct Boston Yanks. He was passing and running out of Giant coach Steve Owen's winged-T formation and received the injury while carrying the ball. "I don't remember much else about that game, except I think we won it," he offered.

I consulted the football scrapbook which I began his last year in college and which is now on the verge of becoming non-portable. A slightly yellowed clipping datelined: Boston; September 23, 1948, revealed that the Giants were definitely the victors (27–7) and that rookie Conerly threw two touchdown passes in his first game. One covered sixty-five yards; the other sixty-six.

The December game with Pittsburgh that year survives recall because in it Charlie set a NFL passing record which still stands. He completed 36 passes in one game—36 completions in 53 attempts for 363 yards and three touchdowns. Surprisingly enough, the Giants were defeated!

Charlie's selection as 1948s Rookie of the Year is a savored memory of those early days.

Another Giant-Pittsburgh game played several years later is remembered with less relish; but Kyle Rote's descriptive monologue makes it seem almost tolerable in retrospect. I quote in part:

"In the opening minutes of the 1952 Steeler game, Giant quarterback Charlie Conerly suffered a shoulder injury. Rookie quarterback Fred Benners was rushed into the breach."

"A few plays later Fred was carried from the field, having suffered torn knee ligaments. The Giant bench was in a dilemma. Fresh out of quarterbacks, Coach Steve Owen scanned the wreckage. 'Okay, Landry, take over.'"

"Now, Tom Landry was a defensive man who, as a pro, had never played offense—much less quarterback. But even in those days he was a discerning student of the game

and had memorized most of the offensive signals in his spare time. You know how resourceful those Texans are."
[Here Kyle suppresses a wry smile, being a Texan himself.]

"Actually Tom didn't do a bad job of running the team, but by now the Giant ranks were so demoralized that the Steelers had a field day. Before long they started to compile what you might call a rather decisive edge."

"I was knocked unconscious in the third quarter," Kyle continues, "but unfortunately I came to, and had to go back into the game. Discipline in the huddle deteriorated rapidly. 'Oh, no you don't!' one player would say, 'I carried the ball last time. Give it to Eddie. It's his turn.'"

"To which Eddie would reply, 'It is not either! I carried twice in a row a while back. Give it to Joe.' . . . And so on."

"Finally Tom engineered a beautiful drive right down the field, and Joe Scott plunged over for the score."

"We really pulled that game out. And that made it Giants 7—Pittsburgh 63 . . ."

For years, when asked to name the most exciting pro game I had ever seen, I said the Giant-Bear game in 1949. Unexpected pleasure is often the most delicious kind. The morning editions had reported that the Bears were favored to win in a fourteen-point walk. Therefore, when the Giants built to a halftime lead of 21–0, exultation replaced the apprehension.

Unfortunately, the contest presently assumed the characteristics of what is commonly called a "good" game. (*My* idea of a good game is one in which the Giants pile up a 35–0 lead in the first half, then roar out of the locker room and run the next kick-off back for a touchdown.) The Bears suddenly drew even, and the "runaway" burst into a breathtaking affair which ended not a moment too soon: Giants 35, Bears 28. Charlie's four touchdown passes were four additional palatable aspects of the day.

It was thrilling; but looking back, I realize that it was probably no more so than any one of half a dozen games of that era. A recent and more detached analysis of the reasons behind this choice lead to a conclusion. For I suspect that the real reason I singled out that game for so long as the finest ever had something to do with my delight over the fact that the Giants, under C. Conerly, had bested the Bears, under J. Lujack.

Johnny was a friend then and is a better one now. However, I recalled having grown a little weary of reading the flood of national publicity accorded Lujack in 1947, his last year at Notre Dame. It had seemed a trifle inequitable that the remaining one percent of nationwide coverage (the approximate amount *not* devoted to John's exploits that year) had to be shared by his contemporaries—such luminous passers as Bobby Layne, Y. A. Tittle, George Blanda, Harry Gilmer, Ray Evans, and Charlie Conerly, among others. After all, hadn't my Charlie copped the mythical collegiate passing title by setting a new national record for completions? And hadn't he led a team that was supposed to finish at the bottom of the Southeastern Conference to the conference title? Notre Dame was admittedly a little better known than Ole Miss at the time; but if the brand of football played in the SEC can't be considered big time, there's not a boll weevil in Mississippi!

I also recalled petulantly that Lujack's college coach, Frank Leahy—as coach of the 1948 College All-Star team—"went all the way" with John on offense in that game, while Charlie alternated with the other would-be passers on defense and did the punting. And after I had traveled all the way to Chicago to see him pass them dizzy! The field announcer even introduced him in the pre-game ceremonies as *George* Conerly.

Somehow I held John Lujack vaguely responsible for this frustrating series of events. Wifely logic works in wondrous ways.

Since the Bears are in the Western Conference, and the Giants in the Eastern, the teams meet only occasionally. Charlie has encountered the Chicagoans four times—in 1948 (Bears 35, Giants 14); in 1949; and twice in 1956. Now there was a year! In a regular-season contest the New Yorkers captured an early 17–0 lead and continued to dominate the action. The Bears got a field goal, but the score was still 17–3 late in the fourth quarter. Indecision suddenly stopped spectators who had begun to file out of Yankee Stadium as Chicago end Harlon Hill made a sensational catch and sprinted for a field-spanning touchdown. Even Giant fans applauded the magnificent effort. We could afford to be charitable; the game was all but over.

Unfortunately, the Giant attempt to freeze the ball and run out the clock failed. With seconds remaining in the game, the Bears regained possession. A unanimous gasp rustled through the stands as end Bill McColl took a hand-off, rolled out, and threw the ball as far as he could. We stared in silence as Harlon made another impossible catch and fell into the end zone. Final score: 17–17. I felt as if someone had picked my pocket.

A rematch was not long in coming, for both the Giants and Bears won their conference titles that year. The championship game was scheduled for December 30, 1956. Though the temperature was between eighteen and twenty degrees, Giant fans soon warmed up to the occasion. Pre-game predictions for a low-scoring game because of the frozen field were wrong. The Giants glided to a stunning 47–7 victory. It was one of those inexplicable days when one team is all fire and the other is all back-fire.

Charlie counts this victory, along with the resulting designation as the World Champions of 1956, as his greatest pro thrill. That evening he muttered over and over to anyone who would listen, "Do you realize we're champions of the whole wide world? That covers a mighty lot of territory!" The din of our celebration was broken again and again by a shout from one elated player or another: "Hey Charlie! Don't forget Afghanistan!" (or "Outer Mongolia" or "Dutch Guiana").

Charlie's sense of well-being lingered long enough for him to purchase his helpmeet an exciting Christmas present—*an absolutely gorgeous mink stole!*

{24}

BIG WINS, BIG LOSSES—I

The Cleveland-Giant series has provided football fans with as many breathless moments as has any other pro rivalry in the last decade—far too many to suit my simple tastes! When the Browns (along with the Baltimore Colts and the San Francisco 49ers) were salvaged from the collapse of the All-America Conference and absorbed by the National Football League in 1950, the sporting public viewed Paul Brown's consistent domination of the AAC with a certain amount of skepticism. "An amazing record," the fan on the street admitted, "but one that was compiled against inferior competition. Wait until the Browns come up against some *real* teams!"

Detractors of the AAC were only partly correct. It was true that many teams in the All-America Conference were pitifully weak compared to their NFL counterparts—but not the Browns. The Clevelanders made the transition to the senior league without breaking stride and defeated every NFL opponent they faced the first year—except the Giants. Despite the fact that before both 1950 Giant-Brown games those shadowy seers, the oddsmakers, had assigned the role of underdog to the New York team, the Giants won over the Browns 6–0 and 17–13: the first time the Cleveland team had suffered defeat at the hands of the same team twice in a single season.

The Giants also finished the year with a 10 and 2 record and found themselves in a slightly ironic position: In order to break the tie for the Eastern Conference crown, they would have to participate in a play-off game against a team they had already defeated twice during the regular season.

Play-off day fell on my birthday, but I didn't receive the present I had hoped for. Playing conditions in Cleveland's Municipal Stadium that bitterly cold day were abominable. The field was frozen solid. A bone-chilling wind swept in from Lake Erie. Light snow fell intermittently. The resulting combination of cold hands and slippery footing dulled the attack of both teams. "It was like trying to run on greasy concrete," end Bill Swiacki observed. In the first period Cleveland's Lou Groza kicked a field goal, but during the entire second quarter neither team was able to penetrate the forty-yard line of the other.

Midway in the fourth quarter the Giants rallied, and Charlie threw a touchdown pass to end Bob McChesney. The jubilant New Yorkers were sobered a few seconds later, as an official ruled that an overanxious Giant had been offside—nullifying the touchdown. Unable to push the ball across again, the Giants settled for a field goal. For a while it seemed that the 3–3 tie would necessitate the first overtime, sudden-death period in the history of the league. However, in the last sixty seconds Groza, who was to be the bane of Giant teams for years to come, kicked another field goal. Then, with eight seconds remaining in the game, Charlie was caught for a safety while attempting a desperation pass from his own end zone. Final score: Browns 8, Giants 3.

In the gloom of the locker room that afternoon Charlie sat, sunken. ("The only time in my life I ever cried over a game.")

In retrospect, he counts the famous sudden-death game with the Colts in 1958 as the biggest disappointment of his career. But I'm not so sure. I think time has merely done a better healing job on the older wounds; for after the loss to Cleveland, I could sense in him a depth of feeling seemingly greater than the one occasioned by the loss to Baltimore in 1958.

Since the Giant-Cleveland competition immediately assumed the anything-can-happen characteristics of a traditional rivalry, there have been many exciting encounters between those two teams in the last dozen years. One of my favorites, strange to say, is a game we did not win—an outing in November of 1955. Rocked by an early 14–0 Giant lead under the direction of quarterback Don Heinrich, the favored Browns roared back with three successive touchdowns. 21–14. Charlie entered the game, and the seesaw began to teeter in earnest. 21–21. 28–28. 35–35. The excitement was almost unbearable. When the Browns lined up for an "easy" twenty-one-yard field goal attempt in the last seconds, I was singularly calm. "They're just not going to make it," I muttered to myself. "A game as close as this just *ought* to end in a tie!"

At that instant Giant tackle Ray Krouse burst through the Cleveland line and batted Groza's kick to the ground. Final score: Giants, 35; Browns, 35. "I told you so!" I told myself.

December 6, 1959, was an absolutely beautiful day in New York, though a dense fog blanketed the field and a sprinkle of rain continued throughout the afternoon. In humbling the Cleveland team 48–7, the Giants handed Paul Brown's Browns their worst regular-season defeat. The lopsided score seemed only to whet the appetite of the partisans. "More . . . More . . . We want fifty!" they chanted.

One Giant player commented: "There is usually no point in deliberately running up such a horrendous score, but we still remember the 62–14 licking Cleveland gave us in 1953, when Brown kept his first team driving until the bitter end." Charlie completed 14 of 21 passes for 271 yards and three TDs, retiring soon after the half as the league's leading passer of 1959.

The rout turned into a riot as fans, exhilarated by success and strong drink, surged onto the field with two minutes remaining in the game. In a frightening display, they tore down one goal post and savagely attacked the other. The comparatively small number of Yankee Stadium police was ineffectual. Cleveland coach Paul Brown wisely made a beeline for the dressing room, and his players unhesitatingly followed.

Realizing that the game had to be completed in order for it to count as a win, Giant players wandered about the field shouting for the fans to disperse. Six-foot-four Roosevelt Brown, caught up in the swirling mass, waved his arms frantically and yelled again and again, "It's Big Rosie talking to you, Big Rosie. *Please* get out of here. Please!"

In the confusion, Dick Modzelewski became separated from his fellows. Suddenly a swarthy customer grabbed him around the throat and began choking him. Dick's not-too-gentle shove served to discourage his inebriated assailant. For almost twenty minutes the field was a frightening muddle of hopped-up humanity. Slowly the crowd (estimated at three thousand) began to melt away. Perhaps the plaintive voice of the field announcer finally made itself understood. Over and over he wailed: "If this game is not completed, the Giants must forfeit, and the Browns will win 1–0."

We held our breath as the field began to clear. The officials dashed into the dressing room and returned with the Cleveland team. As play resumed, the Giants were penalized fifteen yards for "illegal procedure," but the consensus was that the official was trying to move both teams out of reach of the tottering goal post. The Browns held the ball on the ground to run out the clock as quickly as possible. The referee fired the final gun on the run, and everyone streaked for the dressing room. Upon leaving the Stadium, we saw diehard rowdies picking off other recalcitrant strays with bits of the shattered goal posts.

BIG WINS, BIG LOSSES—II

Charlie, as mentioned previously, nominates the World's Championship battle with the Baltimore Colts in 1958 as his biggest disappointment. The sheer drama of the "Greatest Game Ever Played," which featured the first sudden-death overtime period in NFL history, has tended to over-shadow the miraculous chain of events which led up to the Giants' capture of the Eastern Conference title that year.

The New Yorkers were fighting with their backs to the wall from the seventh game on. Every game was a must. The pressure was murderous. "One slip, one lapse, and you're second-best," head coach Howell cautioned his players. "Try not to think beyond the Sunday at hand. Think about the crap shooter who makes twenty passes in a row. It doesn't seem particularly remarkable if you forget the ones past and consider only the roll coming up." We tried.

The Giants' "little miracle" was wrought in wondrous, spine-tingling fashion. They began it on November 2 with an upset victory (21–17) over the previously undefeated Browns, heavy favorites to waltz away with the Eastern title. Surprised, but unshaken, prognosticators once again forecast doom for the New Yorkers in the following week's conference-spanning game against the Colts. An inspired Giant team replied by downing the Colts 24–21, thereby spoiling, for the second time in a row, another team's perfect record.

Skeptics nodded in assent a week later as the Giants bowed to the Steeler jinx in a 31–10 defeat at the hands of Bobby Layne & Co. "Well, that's it. Good try, but they can't possibly win their next five in a row."

November 23: Giants 30, Redskins 0.

November 30: Giants 24, Eagles 10.

The following Sunday, with seconds remaining in the game, the Detroit Lions lined up for a "gum drop" field goal which would have lit up the scoreboard: Lions 20, Giants 19—and dropped us two games behind league-leading Cleveland. Crouched before our television sets back in New York, we Giant wives hid our eyes. But linebacker Harlan Svare came crashing in to block the attempt. Giants 19, Lions 17. Whew!

On December 14, almost blinded by the snow which swirled through Yankee Stadium, Pat Summerall awaited the snap from center. With two minutes and seventeen seconds remaining in the game, Charlie set the ball down on the frozen field, and Pat boomed a desperation kick which split the Cleveland goal posts some forty-nine yards away. Giants 13, Browns 10. Thanks to that improbable feat we were tied with Cleveland for the Eastern Conference crown. Disbelief was unmistakably mingled with jubilation.

Came the play-off game. Shades of 1950. No one had beaten the vaunted Cleveland team three times in one year. Could we do it? Few outside the Giant family thought so, but the players felt they had the Browns' number. They were right.

The only touchdown in that game resulted from a complicated bit of razzle-dazzle—a double hand-off followed by lateral pass. As the play started on the Cleveland nineteen-yard line, Charlie handed off the ball to Alex Webster, who handed off to Frank Gifford. Aided by Al Barry's opportune block, Gifford broke to the twelve-yard line, where he was apparently trapped by three onrushing defenders. Charlie, whose duties as an aggressor ordinarily end behind the line of scrimmage, had been assigned to trail Frank in the event of just such an emergency. Frank hastily lateraled the ball to Charles, who scampered over for the touchdown. Giants 10, Browns 0.

Giant players glanced back over their remarkable stretch drive in the manner of a child half-looking at a scary movie. But the relay was not over. Out of breath? Sorry. One more lap to go.

Meanwhile the Colts, who had sewn up the Western title at game ten, were waiting in the wings—almost languidly. And so began that "Greatest Game."

Leading by a score of 14–3 at halftime, the Colts seemed destined to justify pre-game predictions for a Baltimore victory. Suddenly, perhaps inspired by a goal-line stand which prevented the Colts from scoring in four tries inside the New York three-yard line, the Giant offensive unit caught fire and rattled off two touchdowns for a 17–14 lead.

With only two and a half minutes remaining in the game, Frank Gifford was tackled on his own forty-three—just six inches short of a first down. The Giants wisely elected to punt on fourth down. Considering the outcome of the game, perhaps "wisely" might seem a poor choice of adverb. However, I am speaking of *before* the fact, not after. Football experts agreed that the decision to punt was technically correct, despite the unhappy results. Hindsight is generally more accurate than foresight, but unfortunately, it is not around when we need it most. Since Charlie considered the decision routine, he never ceased to be amazed that anyone could doubt it was the only possible course of action under the circumstances. But so many doubters broached the subject to us in the ensuing months that I perfected a little spiel which I believe reflects Charlie's views on the subject:

Suppose Coach Howell *had* ordered the offense to "go for" the first down, and suppose the Giants *had* succeeded in making the first down, thereby clinching the championship. Had that been the case, I would venture to guess that astute football minds throughout the country would have counted this rash decision as the sports mystery of the century. "Why," they might have argued, "did Howell risk handing over the ball to a professional team within field goal range? He should have realized that the chances were very remote that the Colts could tie the score in slightly more than two minutes! After all—the Giants are blessed with the best defensive unit in the league and probably the best punter. [That punt was fair—caught on the Colt fifteen.] In making the decision to 'go for' the first down, Howell placed the championship in jeopardy. A man in his position should know that such tactics are appropriately employed by a team in desperate straits— not by one that is *ahead* in the waning moments of the game. We shudder to contemplate Coach Howell's fate if his foolhardy maneuver had failed."

End of supposing . . .

Each time we showed the film of the championship game to friends back in Clarksdale, I watched avidly, unable to suppress a faint hope that maybe *this* time . . . But the game always had the same ending: Frank was stopped short of the first down. We punted. Unitas and his Colts drove from their own fifteen-yard line to our twenty in time to kick the tying field goal, and subsequently won the game during the first fifth period in NFL history.

An added un-attraction of the day came to light when Don Heinrich sought me out at our victory-less party that night. "I hate to tell you this, but I just can't stand it any longer. You know the Corvette that *Sport* Magazine awards to the most outstanding player in each championship game? Well, the sports writers had voted it to Charlie and were zipping up their typewriter covers when the Colts marched down the field and tied the score. After the overtime period, they re-voted and gave it to Unitas."

For months afterward I had nightmares about Dorothy Unitas driving gaily around Baltimore in "my" Corvette!

{26}

NOVEMBER 29, 1959 . . .

It was cold and muddy down on the field as we milled about waiting for the Conerly Day proceedings to begin—but being only semiconscious, I didn't realize that until later. My thoughts darted from one subject to another—trying to spot the Giant wives in 24 Mezzanine . . . wondering if Eddie LeBaron was well enough to play . . . thinking maybe the other earrings would have looked better after all . . . hoping that Charlie's sneezing that morning didn't mean he was catching cold . . .

Just then the fans in Yankee Stadium began to stir. The murmur swelled into a roar, and I looked up to see Charlie coming through the goal posts on the far end of the field, escorted by Father Dudley, our team chaplain ex officio. Suddenly sixty-one thousand fans were on their feet clapping and screaming as he walked down the center of the field toward us. I began fumbling in my purse for a Kleenex and came up with a white glove that had been missing since last January. It sufficed. What a moment!

While waiting for the program to get underway, I asked Father Dudley how Charlie was holding up. In reality

I was only making conversation because I was sure Mr. Calm had everything under control as usual.

Father said: "Well, Charlie's a little better now. He was pretty upset back there in the locker room." I was shocked.

As Toots Shor made a brief speech of appreciation, tears streamed down the face of that sentimental gentleman, and I blew my nose on the glove again. My composure returned as the hometown representative, Oscar Carr, spoke. I smiled in the realization that handsome, extroverted Oscar was in some kind of heaven. Yankee Stadium, sixty-one thousand people, nationwide TV . . .

When Charlie closed his remarks with, "Thank you, Slim," I blubbered audibly. Slim is Charlie's private nickname for his friend since childhood, Tony Malvezzi, who was responsible for instituting the Day. The press of business in Clarksdale prevented Tony from attending the ceremonies—or so he said. I rather think he was afraid that if he made the trip to New York, "They" would think he had dipped into the contribution till to finance the journey. That's our Tony.

Afterwards as we were crossing to the sidelines to meet the photographers, Dumas Milner, who had presented me with a 1960 Corvette, caught up and said, "I'd like to have that key I gave you." For one horrible moment I thought he was going to take the car back—until he explained it was the key to his hotel room. (The real key, naturally, was in the ignition switch of the little white beauty across the field.)

Jack Mara, president of the Giants, escorted me from the field to a seat in the stands. As we walked up the ramp, one whole section was waving cardboard-backed "newspapers" emblazoned with banner headlines: CONERLY FOR PRESIDENT.

Among the gifts we received: A 1960 Cadillac from the Giants; the Corvette (got one after all!); a trip to Europe; a movie camera; a Leica camera; a sewing machine, tape recorder, vacuum cleaner, and knitting machine; a silver tea service; two watches; a year's insurance on the cars; a wardrobe of clothes for Charles; luggage; a set of Encyclopedia Americana; a dinette set; binoculars; for the farm, a cotton trailer, enough cotton seed to plant his acreage the next year, and a ton of nitrogen fertilizer; a fishing boat; a transistor portable TV; a sterling silver football of regulation size presented by his teammates and etched with their signatures; and a five-year supply of vitamins. Fortunately a New York trucking company donated its services in transporting the presents from warehouse to Stadium to Clarksdale.

The gift that touched me as much as any other was a gold charm fashioned in the shape of number 42. Inscribed on the back are the words: "To our Perian on her Charlie's day." It was presented to me on C. Day eve by "rival" quarterback Don Heinrich and his wife Barbara.

At the Section Five Club's testimonial dinner-dance that night, Charlie was presented with their Sportsman Award—a beautiful plaque cast in bronze (and weighing thirty-five pounds). The inscription reads: "To Charles Conerly for his distinguished achievement as a football great who has contributed his outstanding ability and sportsmanship to the great game of football which has extended the appreciation of the sport to the world."

That event wound up a day of almost fantastic good fortune. In defeating Washington 45–14, the Giants had put on their greatest offensive-defensive show since the championship game of 1956. Charlie overcame the jinx which usually plagues honored athletes by throwing three touchdown passes before leaving the game at halftime. Both second-place teams, Cleveland and Philadelphia, made outstanding contributions to Conerly Day by losing. Their gifts put us two games in front of the Eastern Conference pack with only two games remaining. No B movie could have had a happier ending.

An incidental pleasure of the occasion was that of showing off "our town" to my mother and to Mr. and Mrs. Conerly, Sr., who spent the preceding week with us. A suspicious regard for airplane travel had heretofore prompted them to decline our annual insistent invitation to visit us in New York. However, I think the actual flight was the highlight of their trip—surpassed only by the Day itself and by having tea with Faye Emerson in her East Side town house.

During the deliciously hectic weeks prior to Conerly Day, whenever Charlie and I discussed it, I had an eerie, dream-like feeling that we were talking about two other people. We can never forget the kindness and warmth of the friends and fans who made this thrilling moment in our lives possible.

Football trophies dating from 1940 (including Most Valuable Player: Clarksdale High School) shine from every corner of our den, but the one of which Charlie is proudest was awarded him just nineteen years later—the Jim Thorpe Memorial Trophy. At the age of thirty-eight he was voted "Professional Football Player of the Year" by his fellow players in the National League.

QUARTERBACK'S COMEBACK

Of all the games in all the years, the two which stirred my emotions to the most painful pitch occurred in 1961. Both were sufficiently thrilling in themselves to rate inclusion among the most memorable in Charlie's career. Placed in the framework of drama surrounding them, they become unforgettable.

Prognosticators had said the 1961 Giants would finish no higher than third in the Eastern Conference. After the initial loss to St. Louis, it seemed as if the seers had been generous. Cardinal red-doggers broke through the Giant line that day—almost at will it appeared—and dribbled Charlie about the Stadium turf like a basketball.

Still, I recalled the optimism among the players when I visited Charlie at Fairfield, Connecticut before the season began. Before I left the training site, at least half a dozen of the players I knew best (all veterans and therefore qualified to make comparative judgments) had eagerly *volunteered* the opinion that the Giants would take the

Eastern Conference crown. "If we can get this thing going [Sherman's new spread offense], we've got the horses [personnel] to go all the way," one player told me. Even Charlie, who seldom waxes enthusiastic, was openly delighted over the prospects of the coming season.

On the basis of my observations that weekend, I ventured a prediction in the first hometown article that the Giants would experience several close calls early in the season, then come on strong as soon as the innovated offense jelled. The prophecy came true, but I failed to foresee that Y. A. Tittle, not Charlie, would be leading the Giants toward the glory of a conference championship.

I was delighted about Y. A.'s brilliant season. However, I must also admit that this feeling did not stem entirely from nobility of character on my part. Even before I met Tittle—in fact, even before the Giants negotiated a trade with the 49ers for his services in July—I was vexed on reading how he had been summarily and publicly relegated to "fourth-string quarterback." In view of San Francisco's new "shotgun" offense, which calls on the quarterback to carry the ball frequently, newsmen naturally wanted to know Tittle's position in the new scheme of things, for Y. A. had never claimed that running was his long suit. It seemed to me that the 49er spokesmen should have saved face for the fourteen-year veteran by offering a noncommittal "We'll-have-to-wait-and-see" answer instead of stating flatly, "Tittle does not fit into our plans at the present time." Having an ingrained sympathy for old pros in general and quarterbacks in particular, I was extremely gratified that Y. A. "showed 'em"—though, needless to say, I would have preferred that his satisfaction had come at the expense of a quarterback other than Charlie!

Later I discovered that it would have been almost impossible to keep from liking Y. A., even if I had tried. He is witty, sincere, and was very helpful in supplying information for my articles. In addition, he liked us (the Giant family) and didn't hesitate to say so again and again. ("I didn't know football could be this much fun!") I was also amused and delighted by his spontaneous expressions of ecstasy at being on a winning club for the first time in his professional career. Since his wife Minnette and I are both long-time members of the Sorority of Quarterback Wives, we had a great deal in common and "hit it off" immediately.

Naturally, I was keenly disappointed that Charlie had finally been ousted from his position as the Giants' No. 1 quarterback, but I derived some comfort from the fact that it took another fourteen-year veteran to do it. Charlie had spelled down many a highly-touted candidate over the years, outlasting all those the Giant organization had groomed, first to assist him, then to replace him. Until Tittle.

As Y. A. tightened his grasp on the starting post by virtue of one outstanding performance after another, Charlie's reaction was to study harder. He pored over his play book at night as if he were the only quarterback in the Giant stable. He was itching to play, but he didn't sulk. Neither did he pretend. When acquaintances sought to gloss over the situation by remarking, "I know you're glad the Giants finally have somebody that can give you a little rest," he invariably refused to let this convenient pretext pass. (Charlie has a proclivity for uncomfortable honesty which I lack.) "That's not why I haven't been playing," he would say. "Tittle's doing a great job, and I'm glad as heck we're winning. But I *want* to play. I just can't get Yat out of there."

As the weeks passed, I found myself dreading the day that Charlie would play. I knew he still had it, but the chances to prove so were to be few and far between. Therefore, it would be imperative that he make the most of each opportunity, if any.

Since Charlie's annual "This-is-my-last-year" avowals had begun in training camp—several months earlier than usual—I suspected that he might be really serious about retiring after the 1961 season. I couldn't bear the thought that he might just "fade away." And so I was torn between the cowardly desire for letting well enough alone and the wish for an opportunity in which he could publicly reconfirm his ability.

An opportunity arose on October 22, the day the Rams came to town. When the Giant offense stuttered and the Los Angeles attack transformed a 10–0 deficit into a 14–10 lead, Charlie flung aside the blue bench cloak. With scant minutes remaining in the third period, he began warming up on the sidelines. I almost got sick to my stomach. As mentioned, I have become increasingly nervous with the passing years whenever Charlie is in the game. This tension is magnified when he is assigned to "go in and pull it out of the fire." Considering the circumstances, on that

Sunday the strain was intense. Though the weather was not severe, I shivered.

The realization of how much his performance might mean was with me so strongly I suddenly became afraid that through thought transference (or whatever students of extrasensory perception call it) I might set him to thinking along the same lines, disrupting his usual calm. Since Charlie lacks my flair for the dramatic, I was certain he had not dwelled on the possible consequences of his undertaking as thoroughly as I had. He looked as unruffled as a T-shirt—and there I was, about to make him nervous through mental telepathy! I berated myself, and told my mind to change the subject.

When the first series of downs which he directed proved ineffectual, an oft-repeated statement of Charlie's intruded. For years, well-meaning friends had downgraded other Giant quarterbacks in Charlie's presence. Instead of taking this as a compliment by indirection (as the speaker usually intended) Charlie leaped to the defense of little-used quarterbacks from Travis Tidwell to Lee Grosscup. "No amount of practice can compensate for a lack of actual field experience. A man who seldom plays loses something of his feel for the game. Even when I miss only one game, I generally find my timing is not what it should be. Imagine how not playing for weeks would affect a quarterback . . ."

I imagined. I even found myself half-wishing the Ram offense would keep the ball just a little longer. Not to score, of course. Just to postpone Charlie's return to action. I even violated my never-pray-for-victory policy and slipped in a little prayer for the "graying veteran" as he trotted onto the field.

"Chuckin' Chuck" forthwith chucked and chucked, and he spun to hand off or fake with an almost boyish agility. At first it appeared that my ESP brain waves had been intercepted not by Charlie but by his teammates. They seemed jittery, as if trying too hard to make his comeback a success. Normally sure-handed receivers like Rote and Shofner dropped perfect passes. But I smiled faintly, for I knew friend Charles was on his way.

Seconds after he passed for the touchdown which put the Giants ahead 17–14, Betty Rote and I turned and inquired of each other in unison: "Do you have an extra Kleenex?" Then quickly we looked away; for I know that had I taken more than a glance at the tears on Betty's cheeks, my own moistness of eye would have evolved into shuddering sobs. And in front of 63,053 people! We were so flustered that we forgot to say, "Needles. Pins. Roosters. Hens . . ." (after having spoken identical words simultaneously). Failure to observe the goodluck ritual had no adverse effect. Exactly two minutes and six seconds later Betty and I were fumbling for our sodden tissues again. Charlie had thrown a second touchdown pass, and the fans in Yankee Stadium were giving him an impromptu standing ovation.

The second of 1961s too-thrilling dramas unfolded in Philadelphia on December 10. The prologue of this script was almost identical to that of the Ram story, for in the intervening weeks Tittle had continued to play the lead handsomely. Consequently, Charlie had to content himself with waiting in the wings.

A thirty-two-yard scoring strike by Tittle via Shofner in the opening minutes of the Eagle game portended sunshine for the Giants on that murky afternoon. However, the Philadelphians stormed back and took a 10–7 lead. The Giant attack stalled time and again as Y. A. seemed to be having trouble solving the Eagles' jitterbugging defense. Just before the half ended, Betty Rote leaned over and almost hesitantly transmitted an unsettling news flash: "Charlie's warming up."

I leaned toward her and whispered, "You think it would do any good if I stood up and shouted, 'We want Grosscup!'?" Those were the last intelligible words I spoke for approximately an hour and a half, with the exception of an occasional agonized "Oh, my goodness!"

I was enveloped by the same personal pressure as in the Ram game, but now the problem was compounded by the fact that the Eastern Conference championship was also at stake. The Giants were tied with the Eagles, and only one game remained after this one. Today's winning team almost surely would capture the conference crown. The losers could look forward to but one sure distinction—five years hence they would be among the few people in the world able to answer this question: "Which Eastern Conference team finished in second place in 1961?"

There was also a little matter of dollars by the thousand. The winners of the World's Championship as decided by the East-West playoff game would net over five thousand dollars each; the losers would receive around three thousand dollars. But first we had to earn the fare to Green Bay by defeating the Eagles.

Charlie seemed both spry and poised as the team broke from the huddle. I resisted the temptation to hide my eyes. In five plays our boys took Giant steps down the field and moved to regain the lead. Noting that the Eagle defenders were double-teaming Shofner and casting suspicious eyes toward Rote, Charlie passed to Joe Walton for a touchdown.

Subsequently he teamed with Shofner for two more aerial touchdowns.

After the second of these, the keeper of the scoreboard reluctantly revealed that the Giants were leading 28–17 with but two minutes and forty-four seconds remaining in the game. "Well, it's all over but the shouting," an Eagle fan near me moaned. Unfortunately, the eleven Eagle fans on the field refused to concede defeat that easily. Wasting only fourteen seconds of the precious time available, Pete Retzlaff snared a Sonny Jurgensen pass and ran over for a sixty-one-yard touchdown. A mere four points now separated the contenders.

The next minute and fifty seconds were the longest of my life. The Giants were forced to punt after one series of downs. Jurgensen hit Bobby Walston on the Giant forty-three. On the last play of the game, Sonny stepped back and heaved one to Retzlaff, who lateraled to speedster Tommy McDonald. For one horrible instant Tommy seemed in the clear, but Erich Barnes raced up just in time to shove him out of bounds. Giants 28, Eagles 24.

Inordinate pride in Charlie's performance, the prime significance of the final outcome, and the nerve-wracking possibilities of the waning seconds combined to leave me weak. Noting that the grandstand crowd had begun to disperse, Betty patted her bruised ribs gingerly (the handiwork of my enthusiastic right elbow) and inquired, "Ready to leave?" I nodded and tried to stand. My knees refused to function. I sat down quickly. The expression "weak in the knees" has a foundation in fact. After several abortive attempts to rise, I was finally able to hobble to field level by clutching at sundry wondering passers-by for support.

As Charlie emerged from the dressing room, he kissed me hello, but it was obvious that his mind was wandering.

"Good game," I offered. "Did you get hurt?"

"No thanks," he replied. "I mean—Thanks. No."

By nature Charlie is restless, but not nervous. However, I have never seen him so wrought up as he was that evening. When our stadium-to-train-station bus became ensnarled in traffic, he fidgeted perceptibly and finally walked up front. He pressed his face against the windshield, as if leaning slightly forward would somehow hasten our arrival.

The train coach occupied by the Giants was strangely quiet. Both the participants in the game and the quasi-official riders were emotionally drained. Charlie paced the aisle, stopping to join a conversation here, kibitz a card game there. He paced and paced. He could have saved the train fare. I heard him mutter under his breath, "Physical? Ha! This game's all mental."

In New York we moved from restaurant to night spot to restaurant. Still he jiggled, unable to remain seated for longer than five minutes. The patrons in two of our favorite haunts greeted his entrance standing. I loved every handclap, but Charles was a mite uncomfortable.

"Am I supposed to sit down, or what?" he whispered. Receiving no reply, he just stood there smiling sheepishly, popping his ankles.

About midnight he began to show signs of partial recovery. "We really won it, didn't we?" he mused.

The sign of relief forming on my lips faded as he continued. "Boy, I almost botched the whole shooting match with that fumbled snap from Wietecha there at the last. I still don't know what happened. Ray says he might have charged forward too soon, but I think I jumped the gun myself. . . . But we really won, didn't we?"

The wife smiled.

Perhaps at least a reluctant mention of the Green Bay incident is in order. I had a good feeling prior to the 1961 championship contest, my intuition insisted that it would be a repetition of the 1956 Bear game. And indeed it was—but in reverse. Once the trend of events was established, excitement was replaced by hope—the hope that it wouldn't be *too* bad. It was.

37–0.

At our defeat party that night Pat Summerall summed up the rather dazed but philosophical attitude of his teammates: "That was the most profitable humiliation I ever participated in."

{28}

THE CONERLY PLAN

Our friends and acquaintances have long since become accustomed to Charlie's Annual Retirement Plan. During the final weeks of *each* of the past ten seasons, he admonished me: "Well, Poo, this is it. You'd better see all the sights and all the shows you've been meaning to see—and do all the shopping—because we won't be back next year. Old Chuck has had it."

Since Charlie has reversed this pronouncement for nine consecutive years, naturally I entertain a certain amount of doubt each time I hear it. I'm positive that in each instance Charlie seriously intended to carry out his vow to retire from football—else why would he exhort me to rush out and spend his hard-earned money? That being the case, what has prompted him to change his mind each spring and sign up to play another year?

I believe that once again the benevolence of Time enters the picture. When he returns to Clarksdale after almost seven months of football, both his mind and body are tired. The closer the race has been, the more apparent the strain. During the last few weeks of the 1958 season, he lost nine pounds. Friends were appalled at how "bad" he looked, and I think he grew a bit weary of hearing them say so.

As the weeks pass, his fancy lightly turns. The rigors and the disappointments of the season gradually become shrouded in a haze of forgetfulness—and the delights appear in sharper focus.

When I overhear him telling an acquaintance that "Training camp isn't so bad. It's not much fun, of course, but it's over before you know it"—I know that within the week he will look up from the evening paper and say almost casually, "I think I'll try it one more year. What do you think?"

"You know I'm all for it," I reply, "but I'm not the one who gets battered around out there." Even if I didn't think he should, I wouldn't try to talk him out of playing. In the first place, he'd probably play anyway. In the second, I've seen the wistful look in the eyes of players who retired solely because their wives insisted on it. As they chat about the then and the now, they play a little game called "It's Lovely in the Outside World." But the eyes say, "I know I could have made it another year or two. If only she hadn't made me quit . . ." And I realize that *she* will never quite be forgiven.

Charlie's tenth pronouncement occurred on schedule—well ahead of it, in fact. This time, Charlie went a step farther than ever before in declaring his intention to call it a career. At a luncheon hosted by the Giant organization in February of 1962 he announced his decision to the press. Never before had he made it that official.

The book is written in the present, lively tense, as if we were still living it, still involved. We always will be.

I'm glad. But as the 1961 season unfolded, I confided to my alter ego, Betty Rote: "After thirteen wonderful years, I can't imagine life without pro football. I know I would miss it terribly. But the games make me too nervous now. They just aren't fun any more. I never thought I'd say it, but I truly hope this year will be Charlie's last."

Old pros think alike, I guess; for as the season drew to a close, Charlie told me, "I believe I could hold up physically another year or two, but I'm beginning to feel the mental pressure more and more. That might affect my playing and it might not, but I couldn't take money for a job I wasn't sure I could do. The life is great, but the games just aren't fun any more.

"For years people have been asking me how much longer I could play," Mr. C. said. "I couldn't answer because I honestly didn't know. Now I do. Knowing when it's time to quit is kind of like knowing when you're in love. It's something nobody else in the world but you yourself can be sure of. Nobody *can* tell you—and nobody has to. It's just something you know."

LAST WORD: "A FOOTBALL FAIRY TALE"

Once upon a time there was a rookie who had just been informed that after undergoing two long months of training and scrutiny, he had become a full-fledged member of a professional football team. He starts a letter home:

Hi, Honey!
The coach made the final cuts today, and I made the team! Imagine—the big leagues! I want you and the baby to come up as soon as possible. I've gotten us an apartment in the hotel where most of the other fellows and their families will be staying during the season. Hurry on up. I miss you.
P.S. Be sure to tell Old Joe and the rest of the gang my good news. . . .

His little family arrives. Later, at one of the informal team gatherings, he falls into a conversation that will not vary more than two words from the following: *"I plan to play only one year—perhaps two—to get enough money for a house (and/or business) and then quit in order to establish my real career."*

The listener nods politely as if hearing this familiar statement for the first time. Such optimism, though admirable, is ill-fated. To illustrate these silent musings with a bit of pirated verse:

It takes a heap of living to make a house a home,
And it takes a lot of football to make a house your own . . .

The dreamer is first jolted when he realizes that the cost of moving his family temporarily to the city of play grossly exceeds his expectations. Experiments in leaving them behind backfire—financially, because of the cost of maintaining two residences, and emotionally, because of prolonged separation (a total of five months—two of training and three of the actual season). *"And while we're in the city we might as well take advantage of the wonderful opportunities here. We might never get back."*

When the season ends, the happy little family returns to the hometown. *"But suppose the transplanting did make a mess of our budget. Look how much we have left! I'll bet Old Joe doesn't make that much in a whole year."*

The listener tactfully refrains from reminding him that Old Joe just keeps plugging away for twelve months—and draws twelve months' salary in the doing.

Our rookie is further startled by the fact that although the local businessmen enjoy hearing about his exploits, an occasional free lunch at the Rotary Club is sometimes his only tangible benefit.

"And whatever happened to those 'good business connections' everybody said I'd make?"

The listener could point out that one can hardly blame an employer for being reluctant to undergo the expense of training a man for a job, or simply hiring one, knowing that he will be available for duty only half the year. And so it is not unusual for our rookie to sit out the off-season watching the dream of a paid-in-full deed to the new house dwindle to "a substantial down payment."

Time goes on. One day our friend is astounded to discover that instead of a callow first-year man, he is now a veteran of five—eight—even fourteen years! What could possibly have made him waver from his original strong resolution. Money? Only partly.

The months and years of thinking as a team foster an all-for-one fellowship that often ripens into deep and lasting friendship—as evidenced by the sometimes staggering off-season phone bills to places like Bakersfield, California, or Upper Sandusky, Ohio, or Cedartown, Georgia.

There is also the rewarding experience of travel. The excitement of meeting famous people. The secret, rosy glow engendered by the thrill of being a "name." Of being recognized on the street. Of signing autographs for adoring youngsters. Of being claimed as kin by eleventh cousins.

But most important of all: He loves to play the game. He simply could not endure the physical and mental severity were the game of football not in his blood. It is an incurable disease—a compulsive ailment of the mind and heart. It is also highly contagious. And as you might have guessed, members of a player's immediate family are particularly susceptible to this marvelous malady.

AFTERWORD

It all seems so quaint now—this *Backseat Quarterback* written so many years ago. Forty? Not possible!

In those succeeding years, Charlie and I had a very interesting, satisfying life full of friendships, travel, and several business ventures—the most successful being a chain of eight Conerly Shoe Stores in Mississippi. About fifteen years ago, we sold the stores to his best friend and partner, Tony Malvezzi, whose five children have afforded us such immense pleasure down through the years.

Charlie's number 42 was retired by the Giants in 1962. In 1968, he was elected to the National College Football Hall of Fame. He was named to the Ole Miss Team of the Century (1893–1992).

During the sixties and early seventies and perhaps beyond (I've forgotten), Charlie was the Marlboro Man. His picture appeared on billboards, in magazines, in newspapers, and on TV when that was allowed. His name did not appear because he was a model, not an endorser of the cigarette—as he was always quick to point out. But, yes, he did smoke. Marlboros, of course. And yes, he finally quit.

Each fall Charlie and I went to the Ole Miss home games and picnicked in The Grove. (I still do.) We also took in several Giants games in New York each year— sitting in the Mara family box. Incredibly wonderful people, those Maras!

Ever lean and lithe, Charlie was a neighborhood fixture as he briskly walked his daily two miles, rain or shine.

In later years when his golf game lagged and he quit playing with the "big boys," Charlie and I played nine holes almost every afternoon late, weather permitting.

We kept up with a lot of the old Giants—Frank Gifford, Pat Summerall, Rosie Brown, Harland Svare, Alex Webster, Ray Beck, Dick Lynch, Kyle Rote, and of course, the Mississippi Poole brothers, Ray and Barney. And with the Giants owners, Wellington Mara and Timmy Mara.

Charlie died in 1996 of complications following heart surgery. Later that year, our godchild, Lulu, instigated the creation of the Conerly Trophy, awarded each year to the best collegiate player in Mississippi. (There are ten four-year colleges in the state that play football.) Some of the speakers at the annual December presentation include Frank Gifford, Jack Kemp (the year he ran for vice president), Pat Summerall, Tom Landry, and Bart Starr.

As for me:

I do a bit of traveling. Actually, I do a lot of traveling. I play bridge. I have good friends, and people here are thoughtful about including widows in fun events. Two marvelous cats, Bubba and Miss Callie, keep me entertained in my down time.

In December 2002, I moved into a wonderful house nearer the golf course, and I play (badly) several times a week with a group of guys—most of whom I went to high school with.

Incidentally, when I moved, I ran across a box of "stuff" that Charlie's mother had passed along. In it was the mangled clip from the rifle that was shot out of Charlie's hand by a Japanese sniper on Guam in 1944—also the letter from the Navy Department to his parents detailing the incident. Though he was proud to have been a Marine, Charlie would have been embarrassed that I now have those particular objects prominently displayed. I can just imagine him raking them quietly into a drawer.

I miss Charlie every day. But I'm okay.

Perian
2003

Printed in the United States
by Baker & Taylor Publisher Services